God is Love

COLOR 60 INSPIRATIONAL BIBLE VERSES

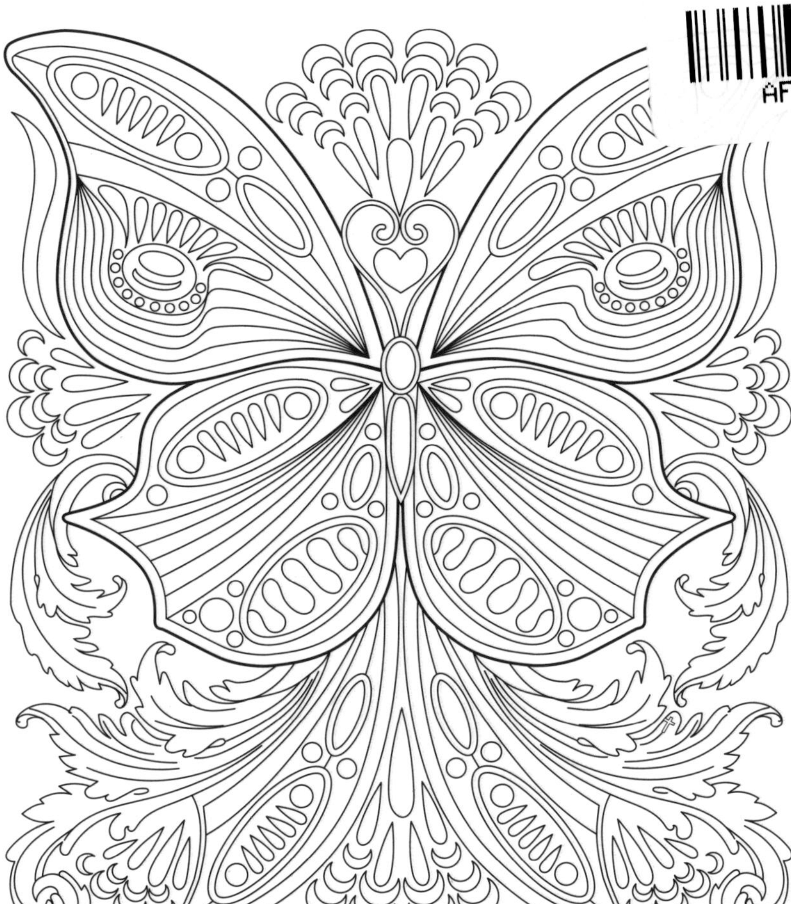

PAMELA THAYER

Get Creative 6
NEW YORK

This book is dedicated to my husband of 47 years, Charles T. Thayer (3/12/54–8/13/21).

Get Creative 6
An imprint of Mixed Media Resources
19 West 21st Street
Suite 601
New York, New York 10010

Editor
LAUREN O'NEAL

Creative Director
IRENE LEDWITH

Designer
JENNIFER MARKSON

Chief Executive Officer
CAROLINE KILMER

President
ART JOINNIDES

Chairman
JAY STEIN

ISBN: 978-1-68462-052-4

Manufactured in China

3 5 7 9 10 8 6 4

A NOTE FROM THE AUTHOR

As you color the images in this book, please know that you are loved by the Creator of the universe. Each illustration here contains a tiny cross. It's a subtle reminder that if you seek the cross and Christ in your life, all else will fall into place. I hope that coloring these images brings you as much joy as I experienced while creating them.

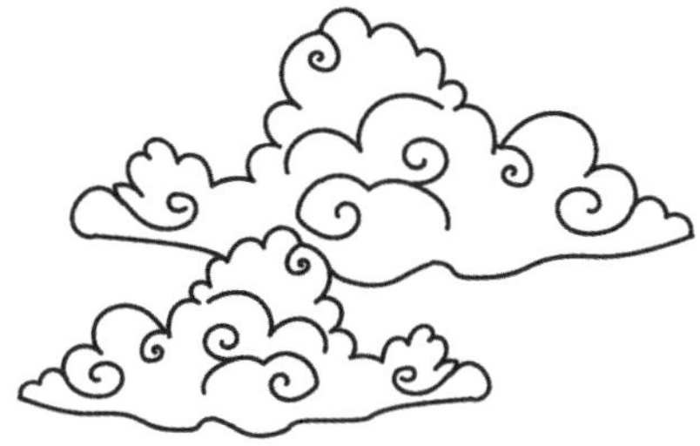

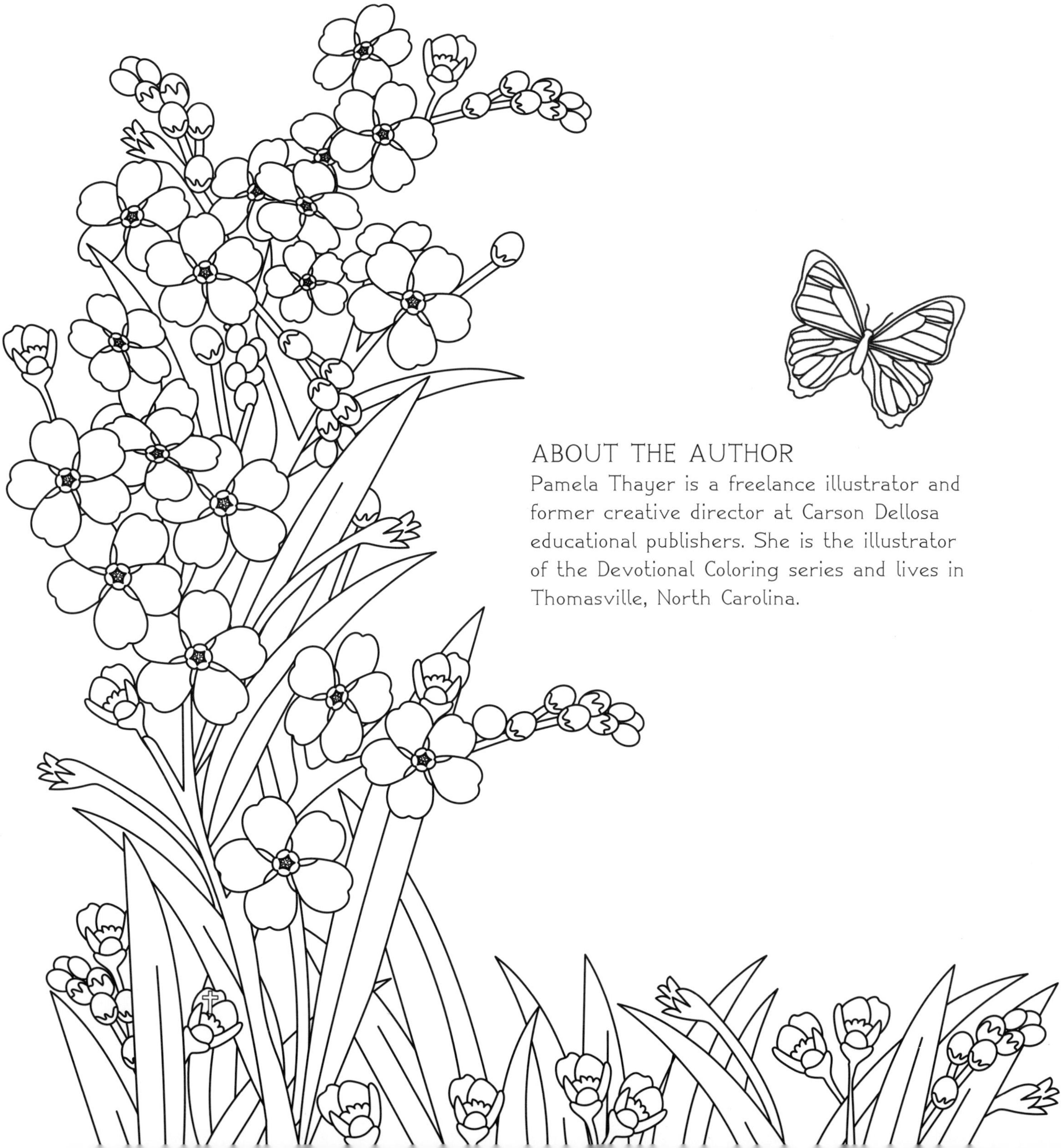

ABOUT THE AUTHOR

Pamela Thayer is a freelance illustrator and former creative director at Carson Dellosa educational publishers. She is the illustrator of the Devotional Coloring series and lives in Thomasville, North Carolina.

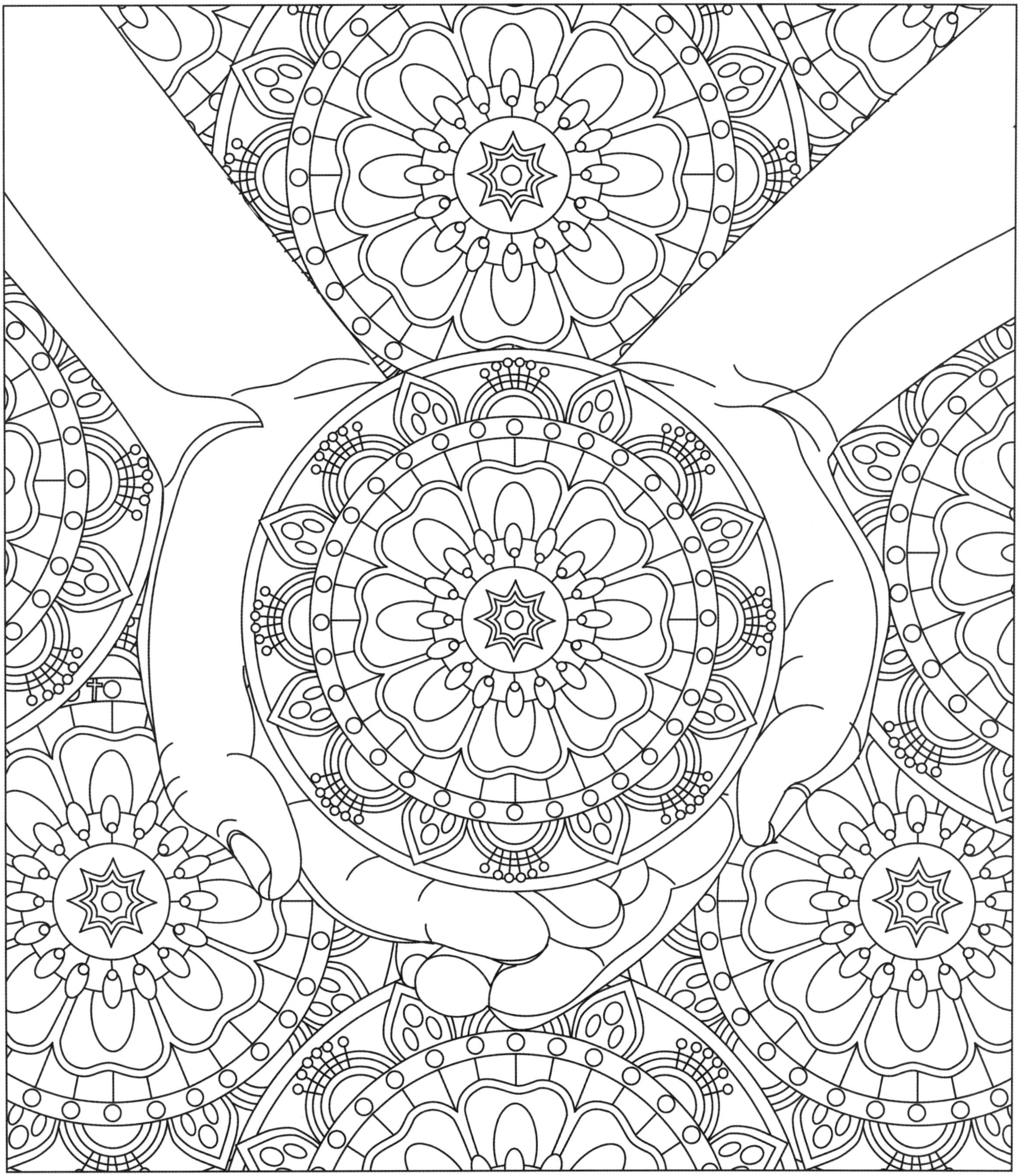

Let all your things be done with charity.
1 Corinthians 16:14

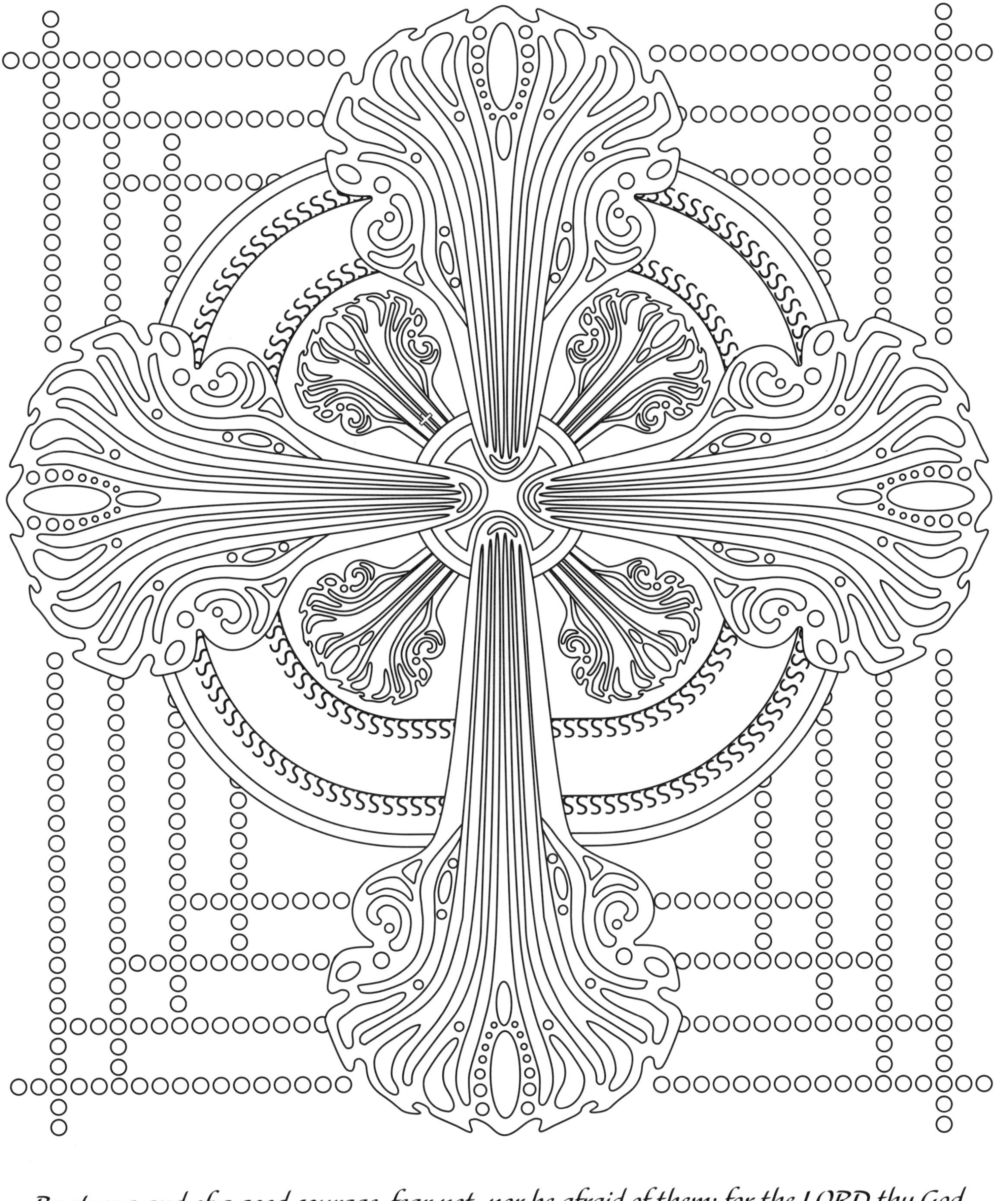

Be strong and of a good courage, fear not, nor be afraid of them: for the LORD thy God, he [it is] that doth go with thee; he will not fail thee,nor forsake thee.

Deuteronomy 31:6

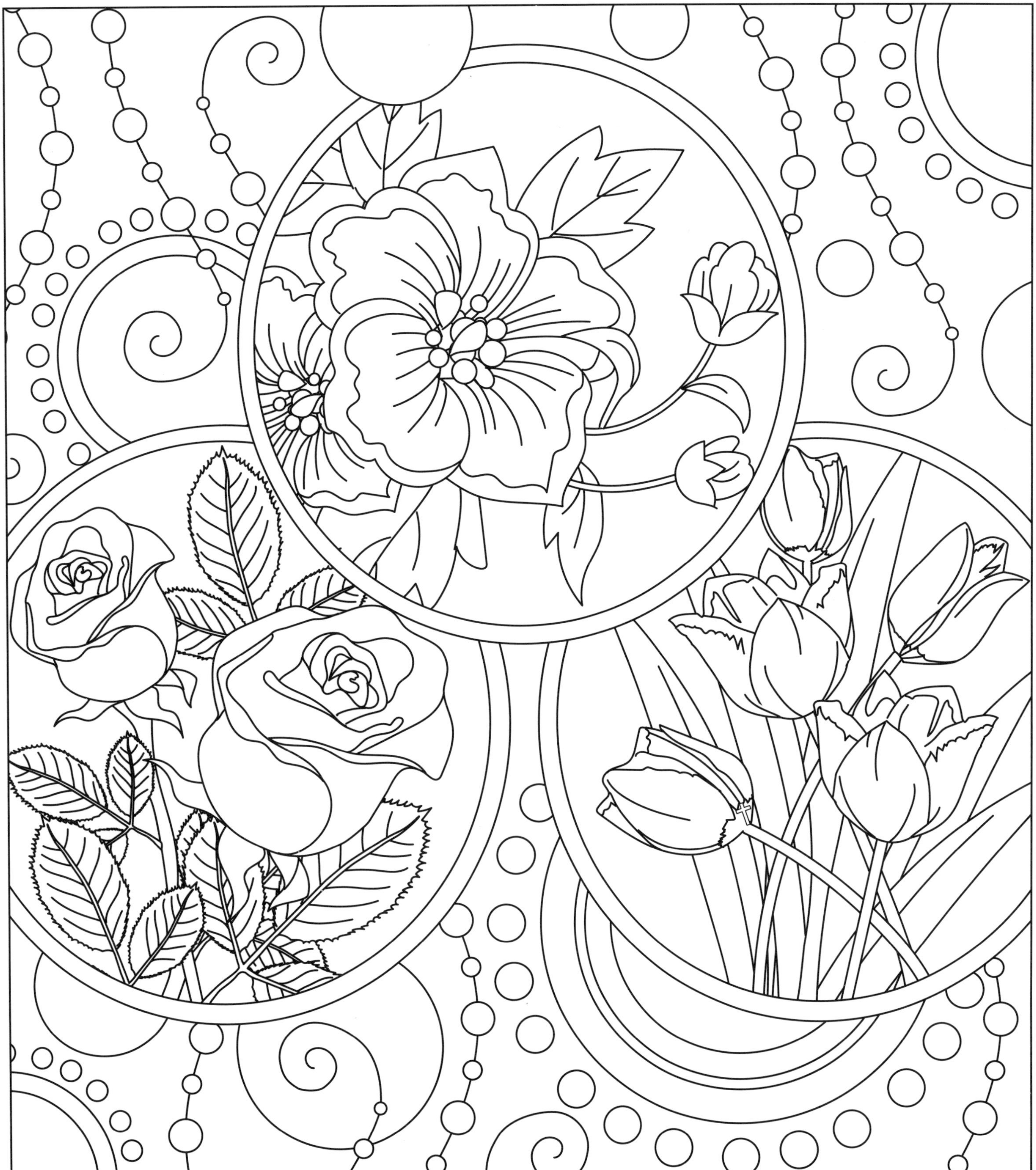

But the mercy of the LORD [is] from everlasting to everlasting upon them that fear him, and his righteousness unto children's children.

Psalm 103:17

Thy word have I hid in mine heart, that I might not sin against thee.

Psalm 119:11

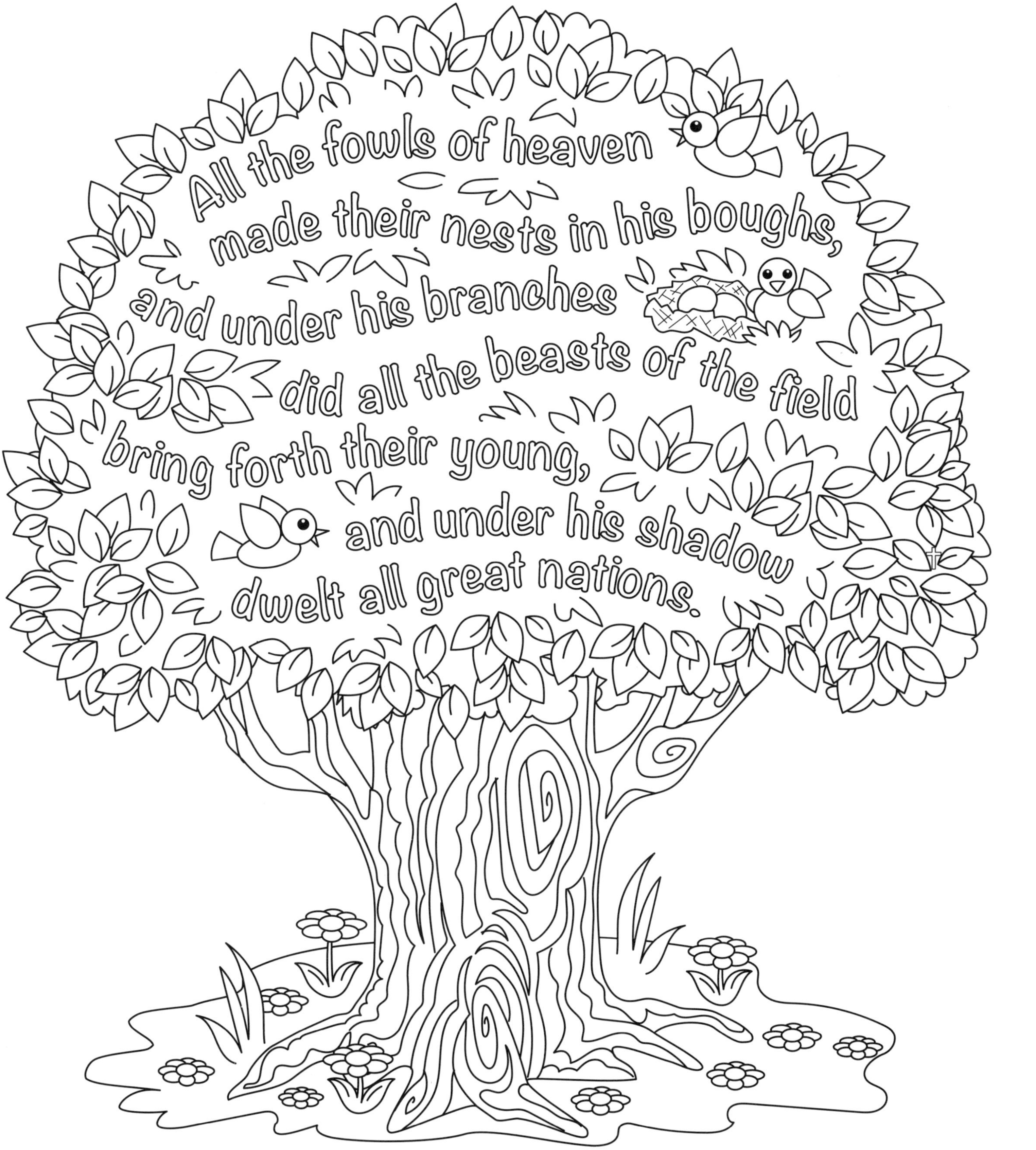

All the fowls of heaven made their nests in his boughs, and under his branches did all the beasts of the field bring forth their young, and under his shadow dwelt all great nations.

Ezekiel 31:6

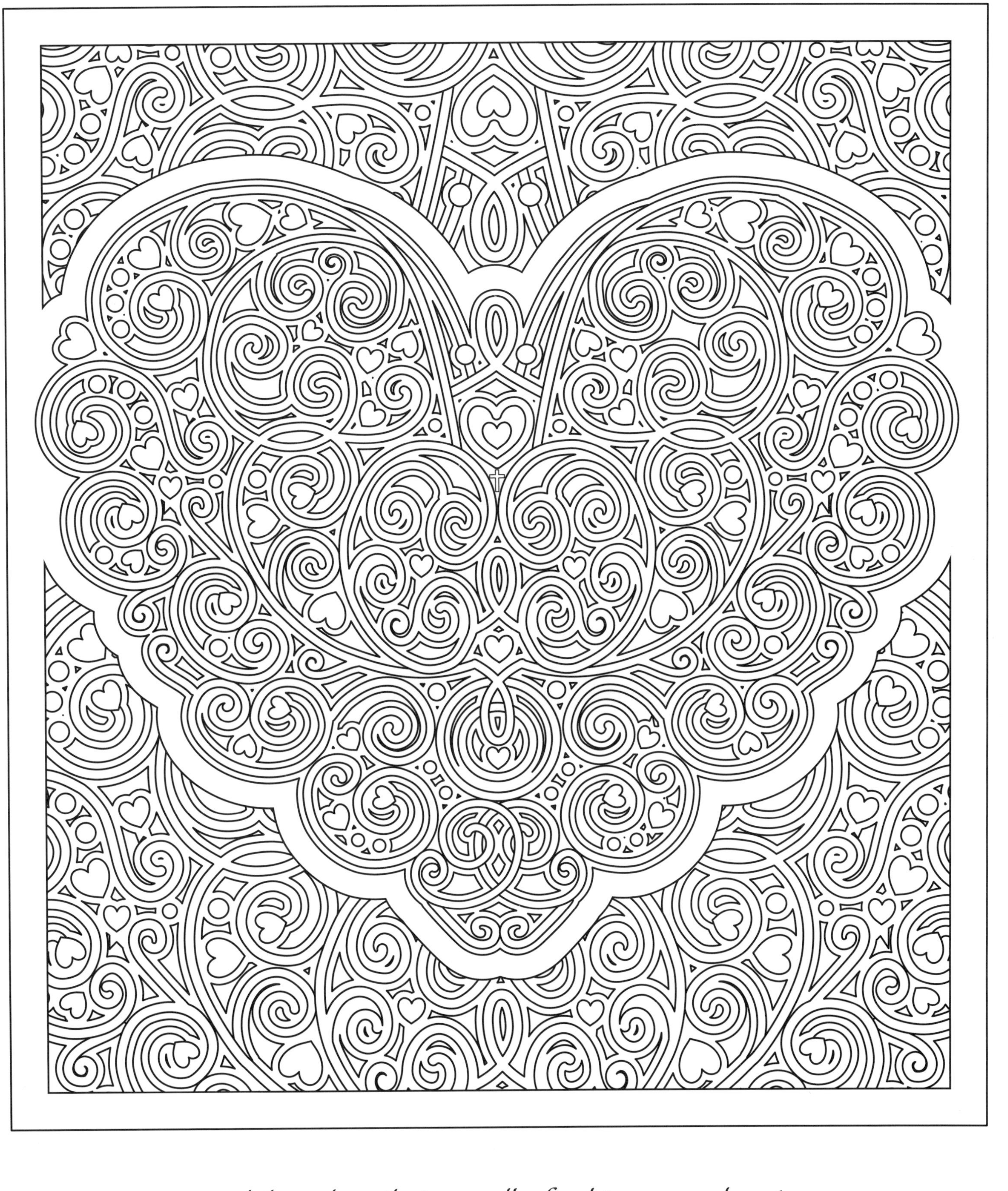

And this is love, that we walk after his commandments.
2 John 1:6

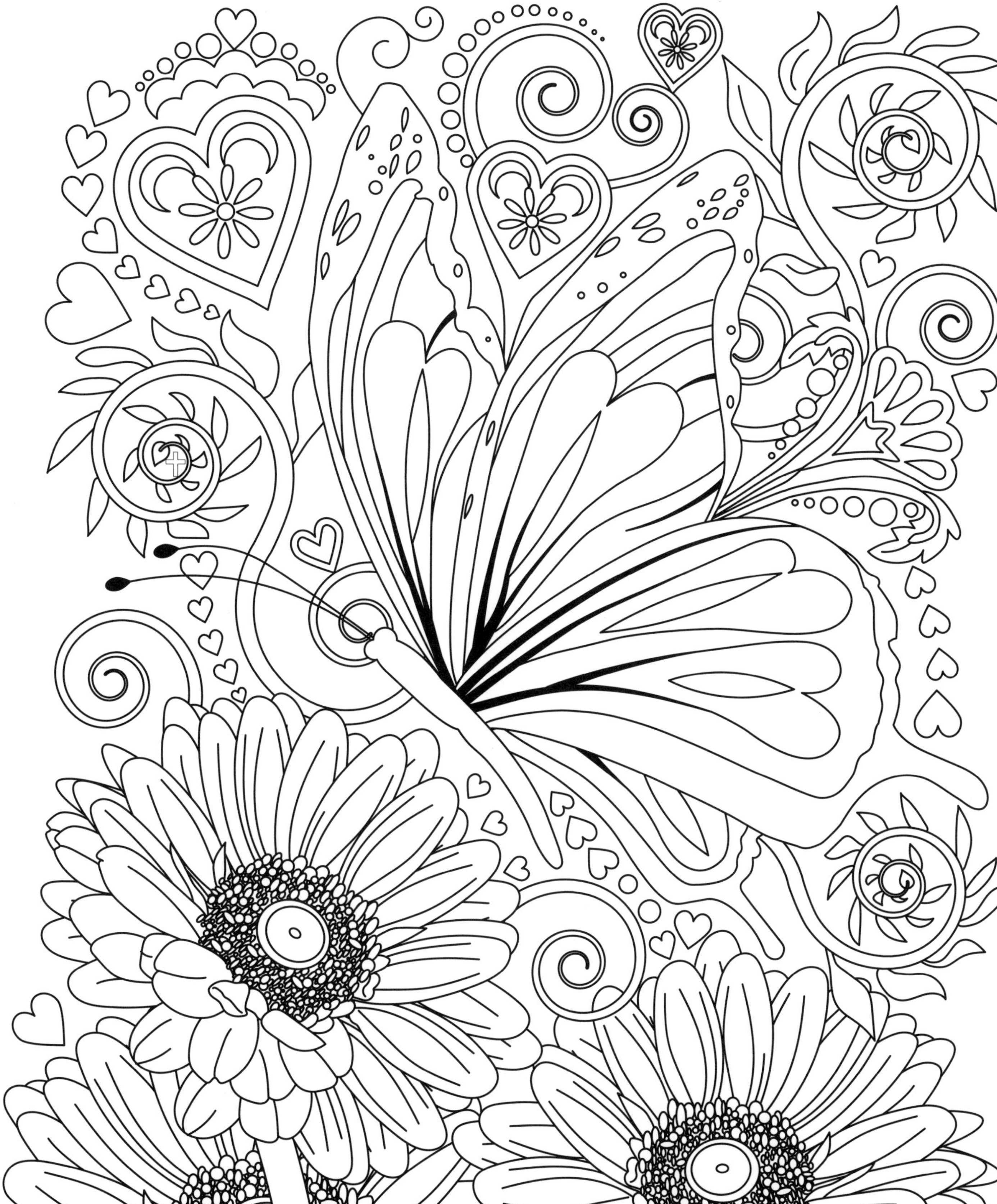

He hath made every thing beautiful in his time.
Ecclesiastes 3:11

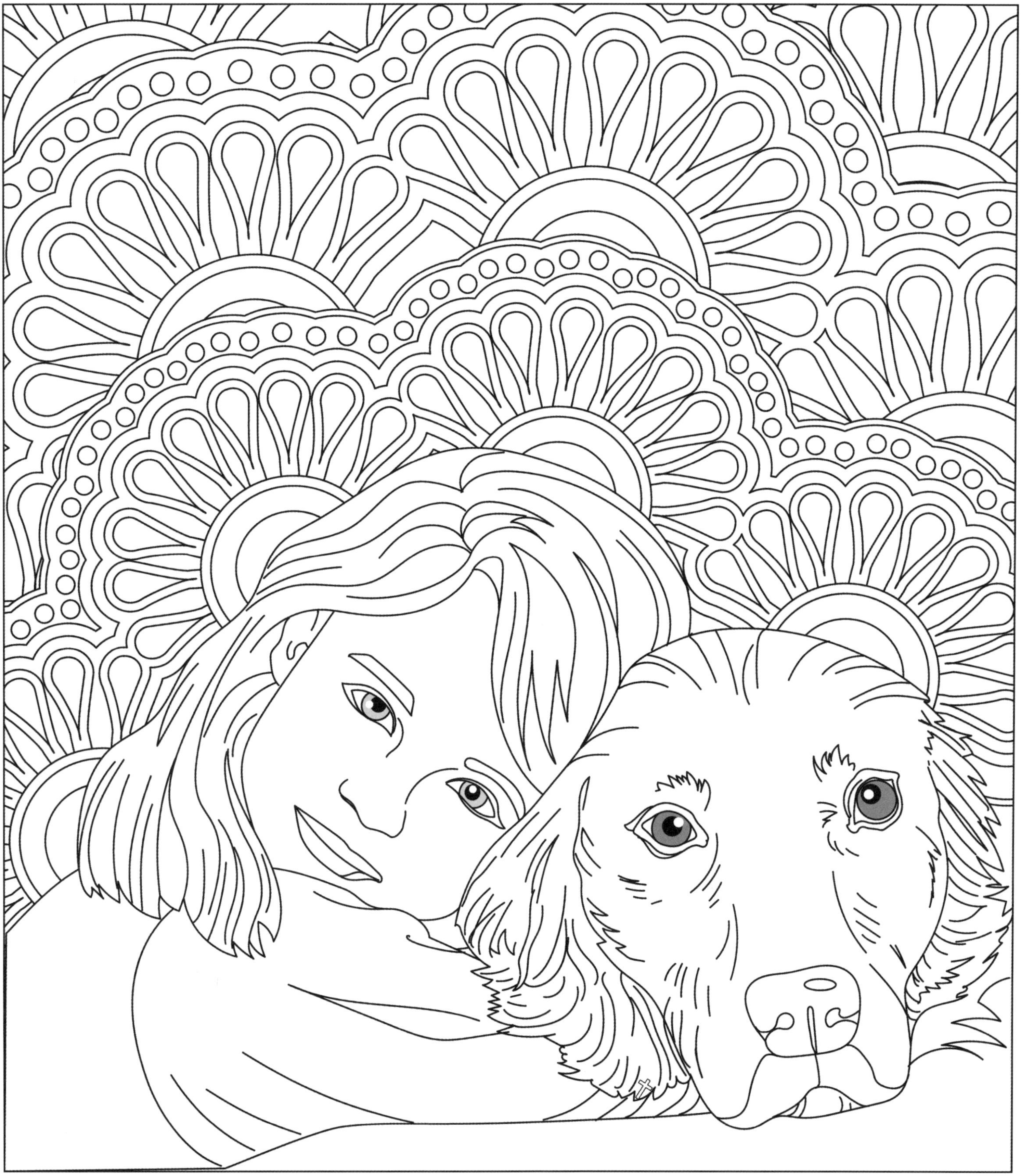

Fear thou not; for I [am] with thee: be not dismayed; for I [am] thy God: I will strengthen thee; yea, I will help thee; yea, I will uphold thee with the right hand of my righteousness.

Isaiah 41:10

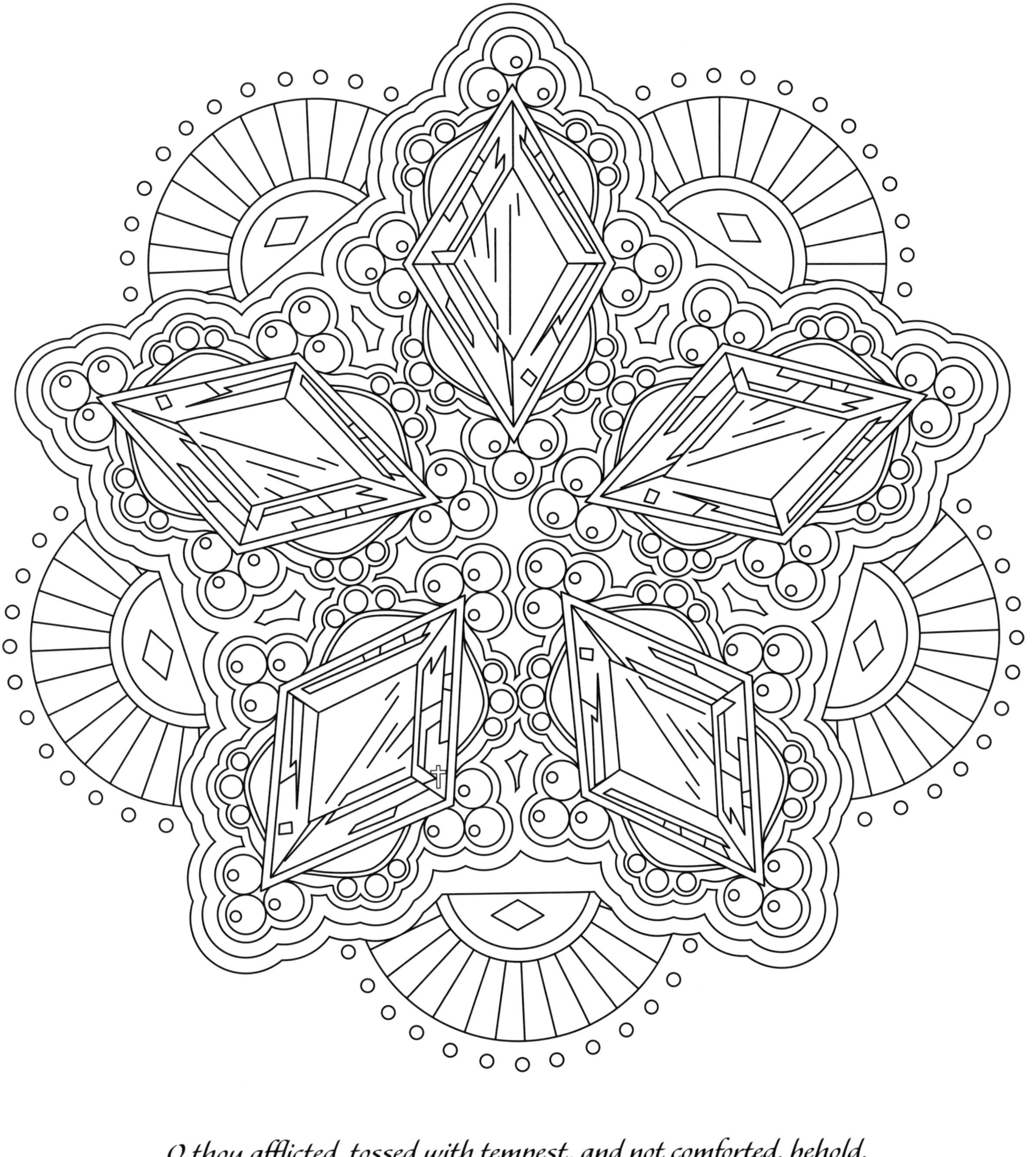

O thou afflicted, tossed with tempest, and not comforted, behold,
I will lay thy stones with fair colours,
and lay thy foundations with sapphires.
Isaiah 54:11

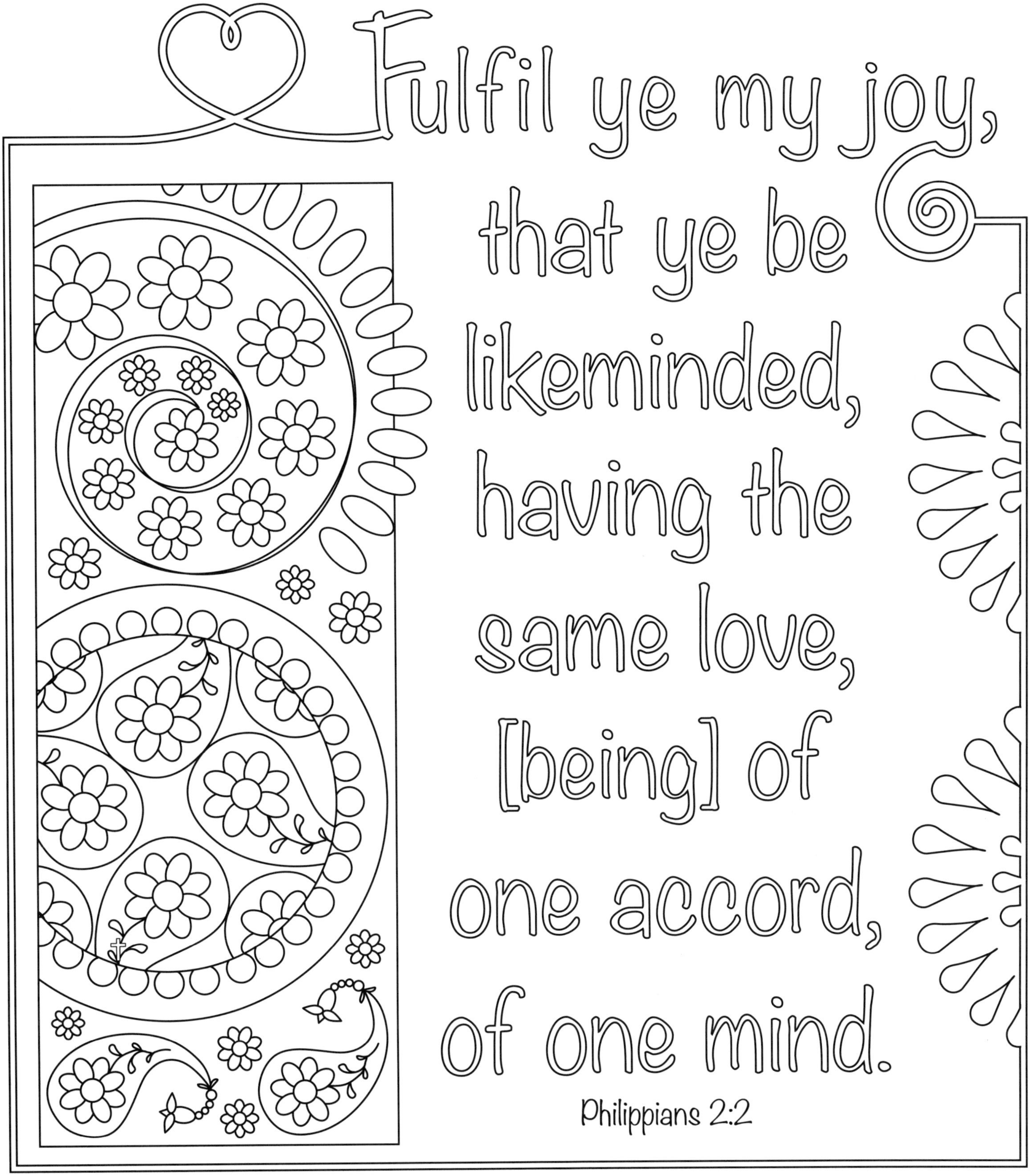

Fulfil ye my joy, that ye be likeminded, having the same love,
[being] of one accord, of one mind.
Philippians 2:2

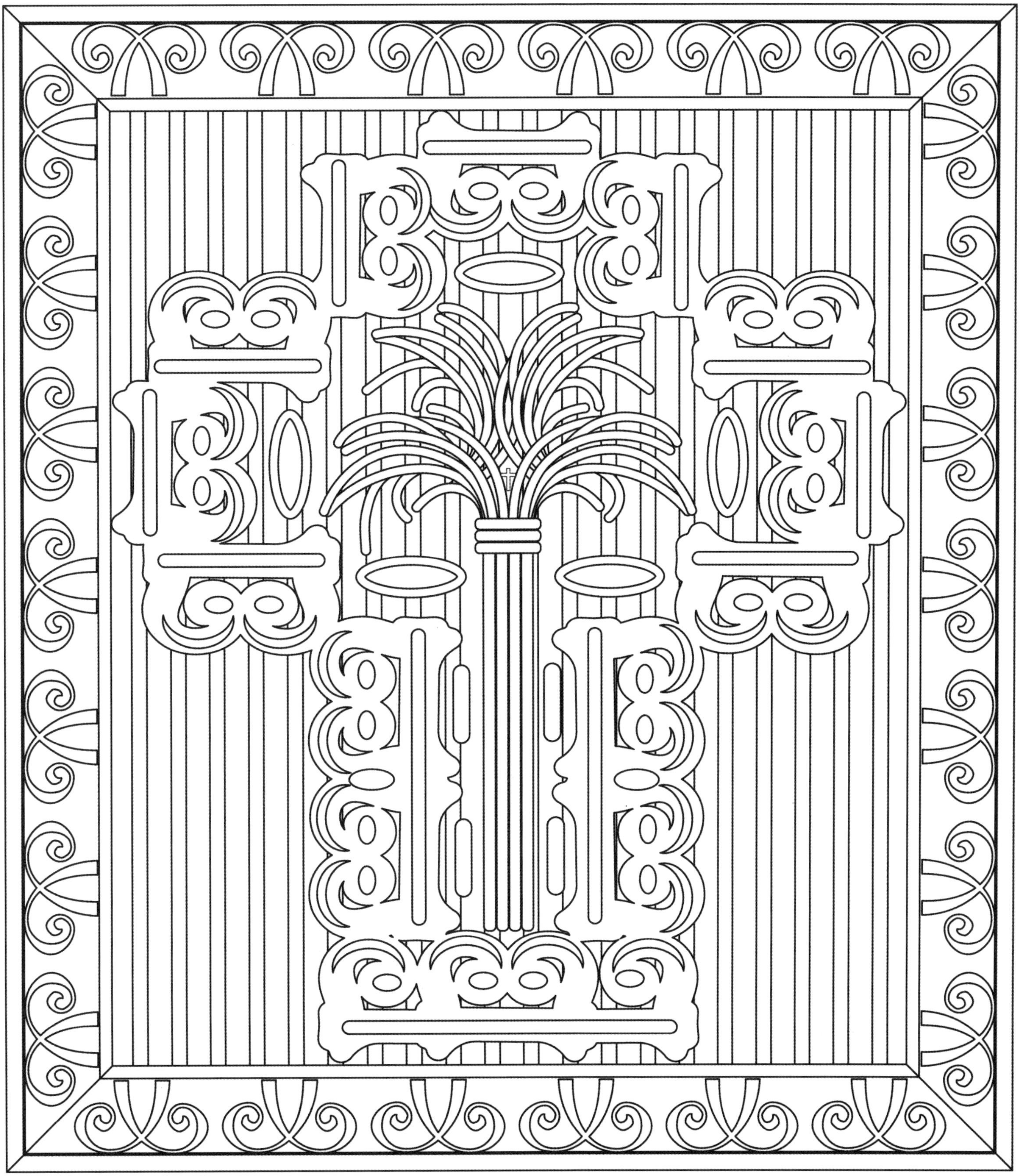

Behold, God [is] my salvation; I will trust, and not be afraid: for the LORD JEHOVAH [is] my strength and [my] song; he also is become my salvation.

Isaiah 12:2

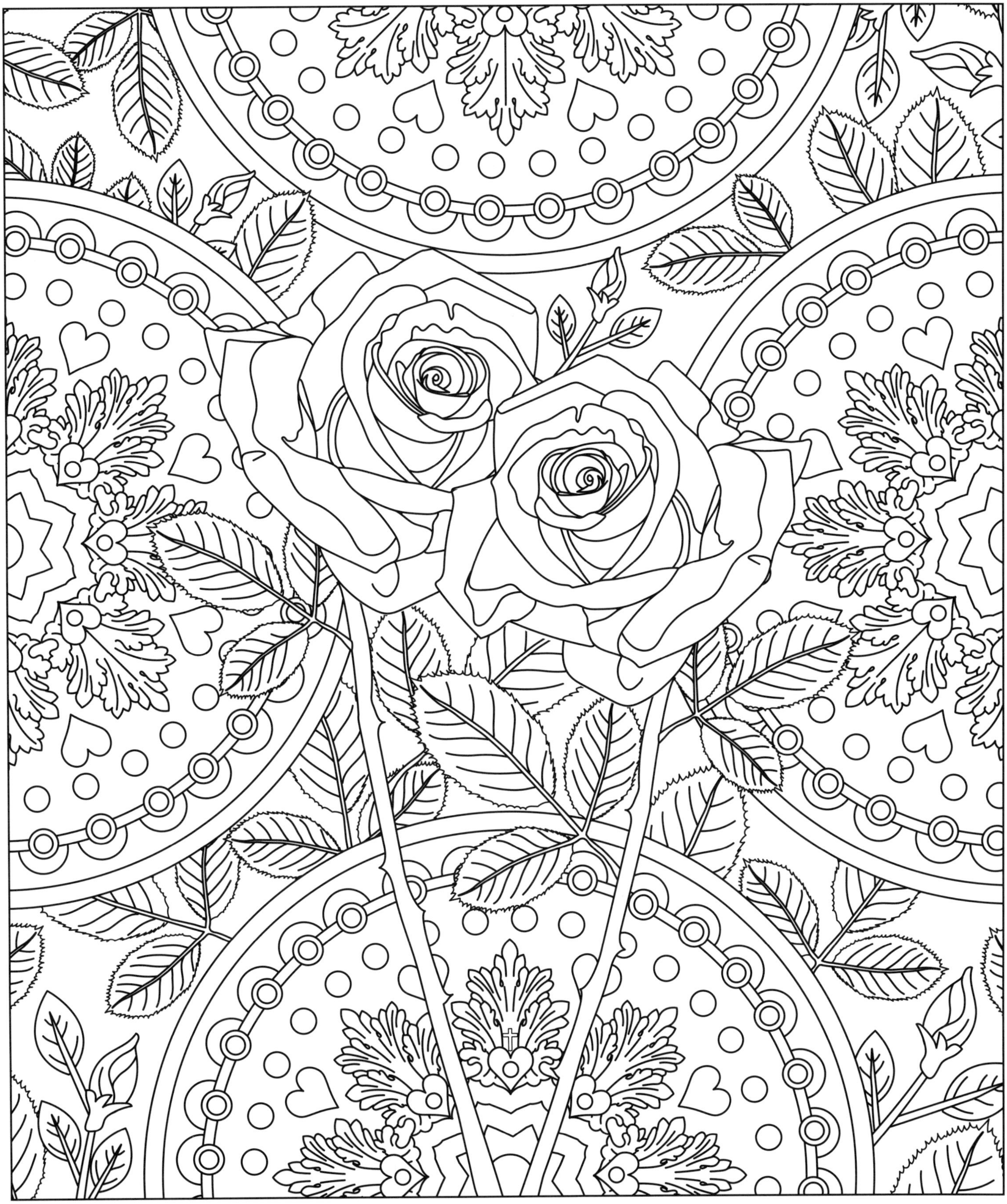

Beloved, let us love one another: for love is of God;
and every one that loveth is born of God, and knoweth God.
1 John 4:7

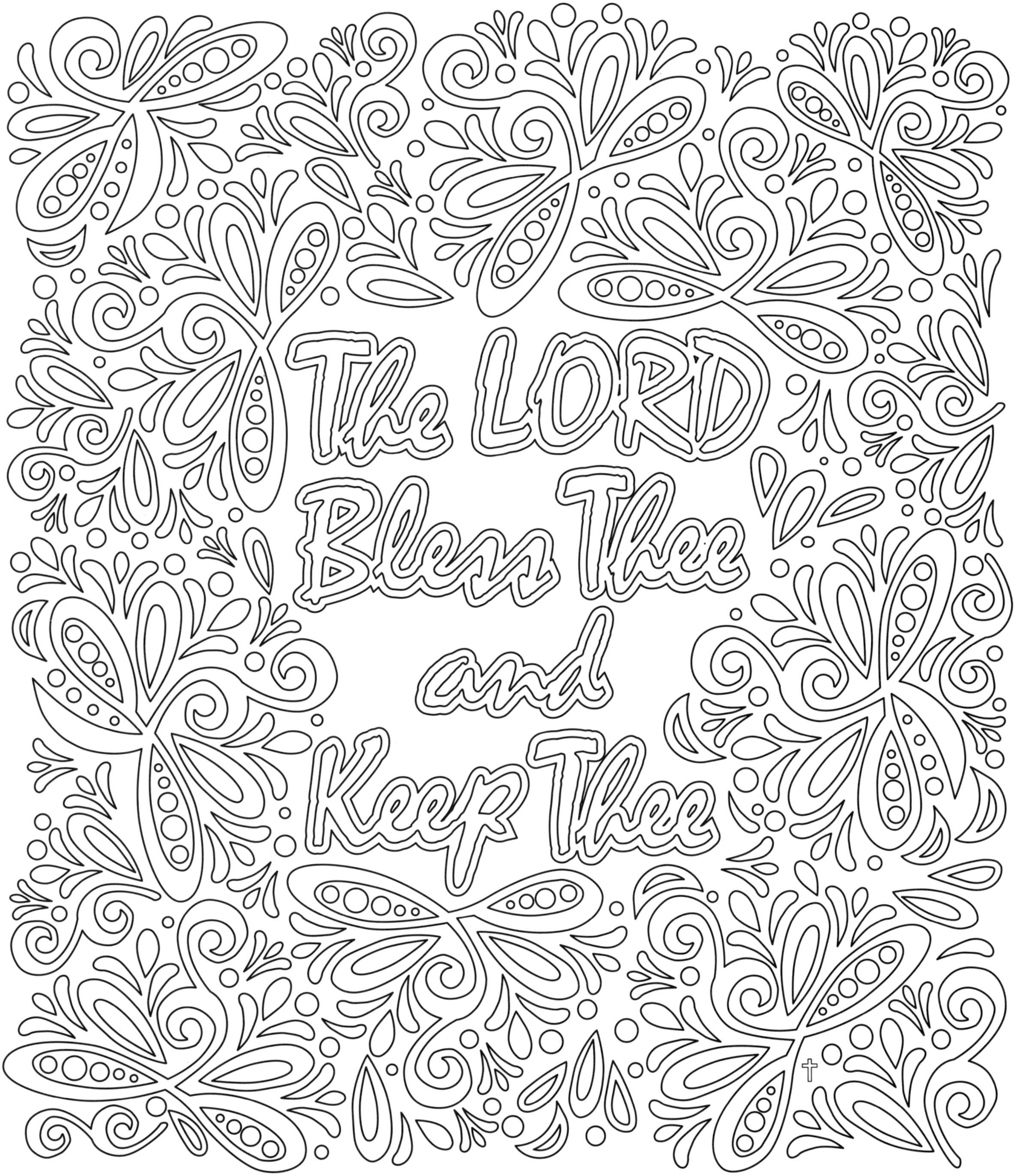

The LORD bless thee, and keep thee.

Numbers 6:24

Glory ye in his holy name: let the heart of them rejoice that seek the LORD.
1 Chronicles 16:10

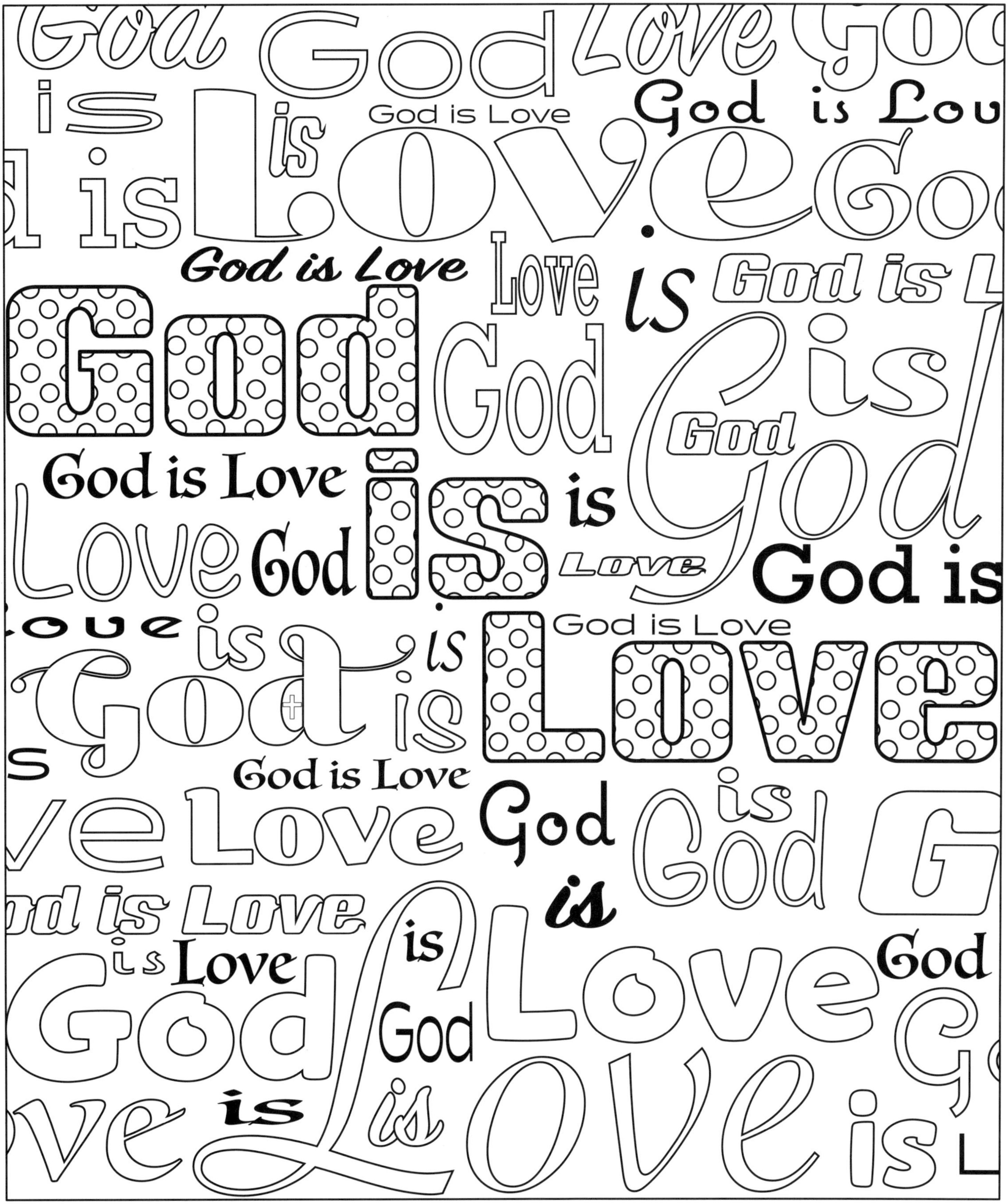

The LORD my God will enlighten my darkness.

Psalm 18:28

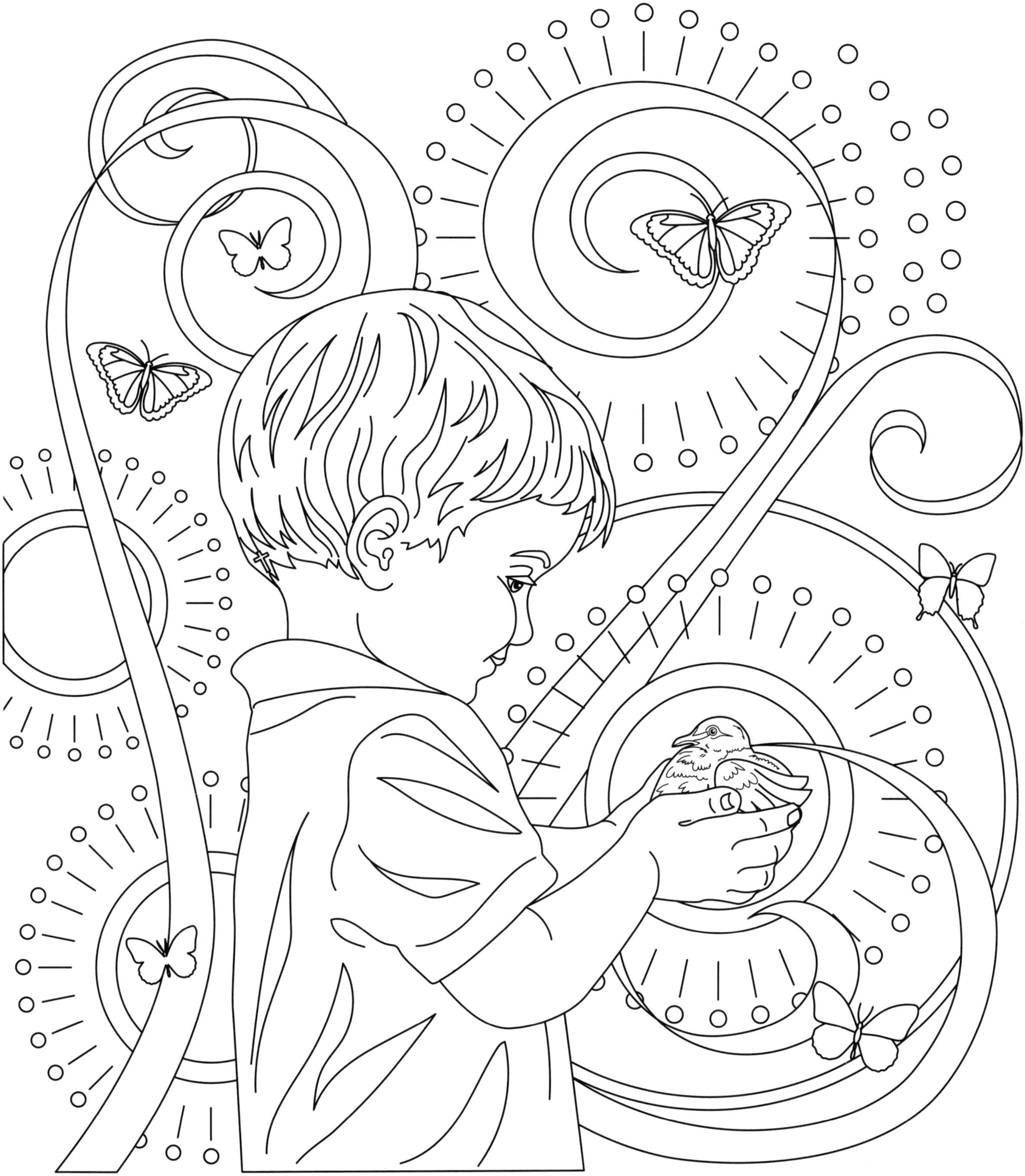

Even a child is known by his doings, whether his work [be] pure, and whether [it be] right.

Proverbs 20:11

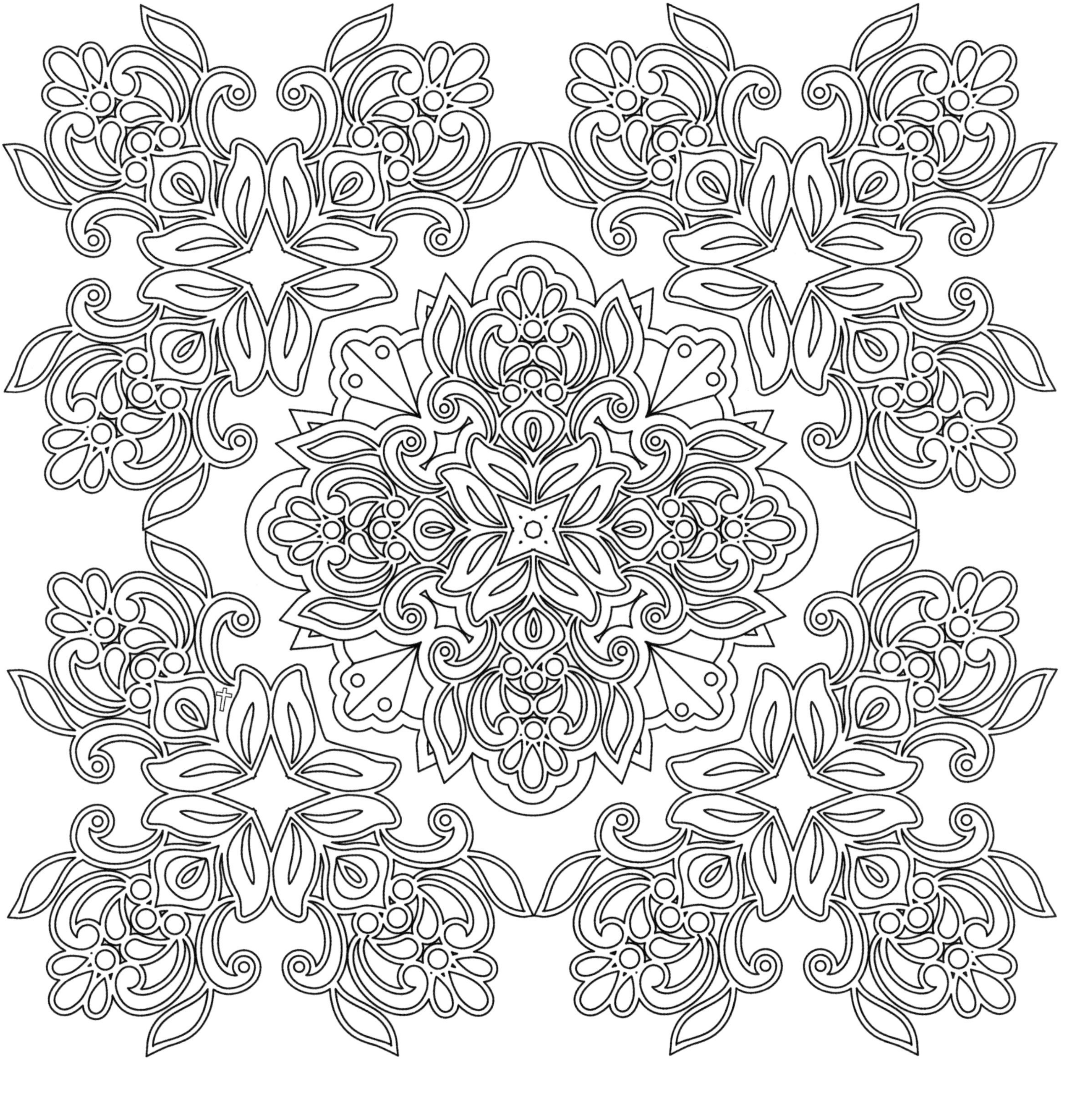

Rejoicing in hope; patient in tribulation; continuing instant in prayer...
Romans 12:12

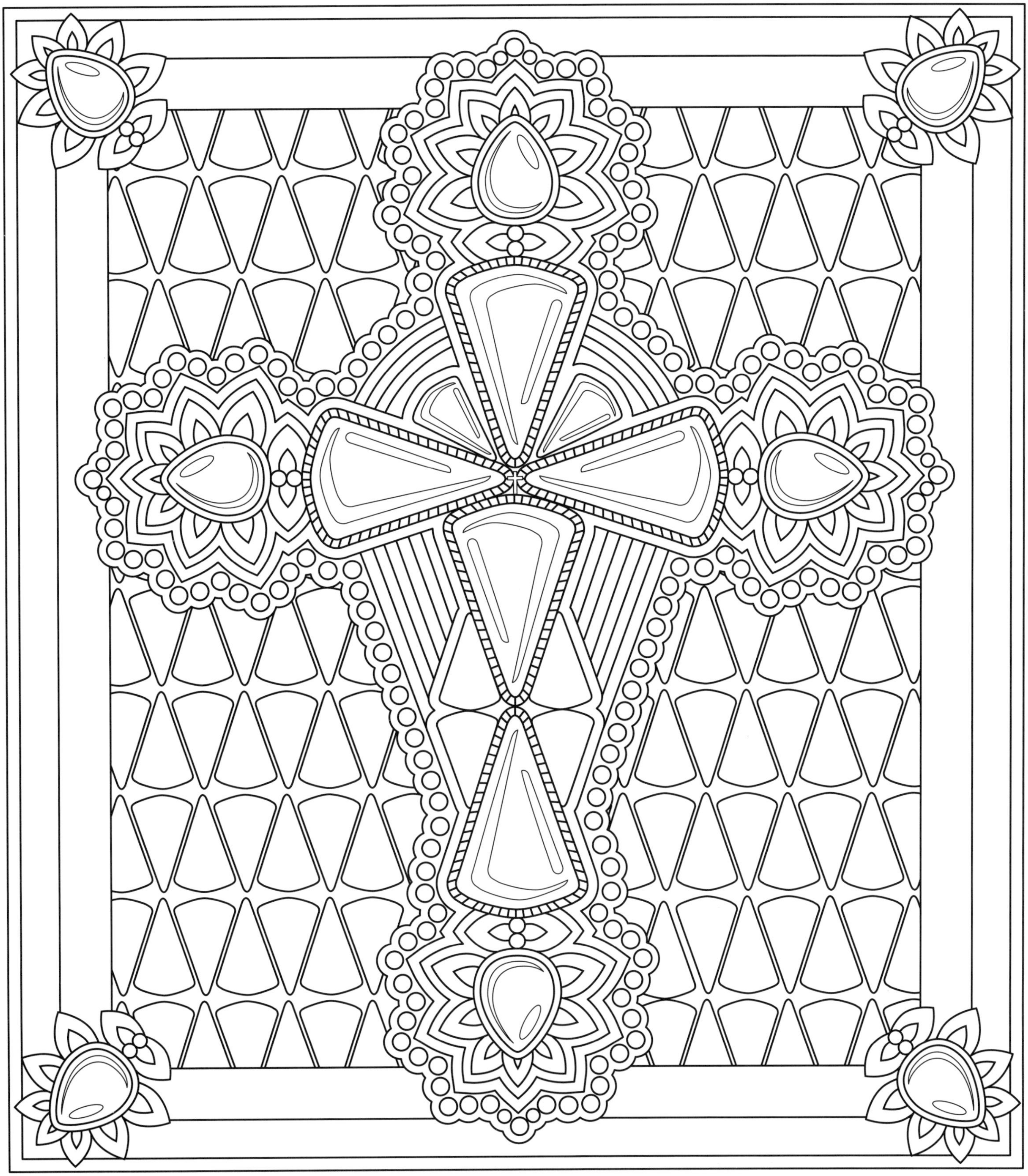

God [is] faithful, by whom ye were called unto the fellowship of his Son Jesus Christ our Lord.

1 Corinthians 1:9

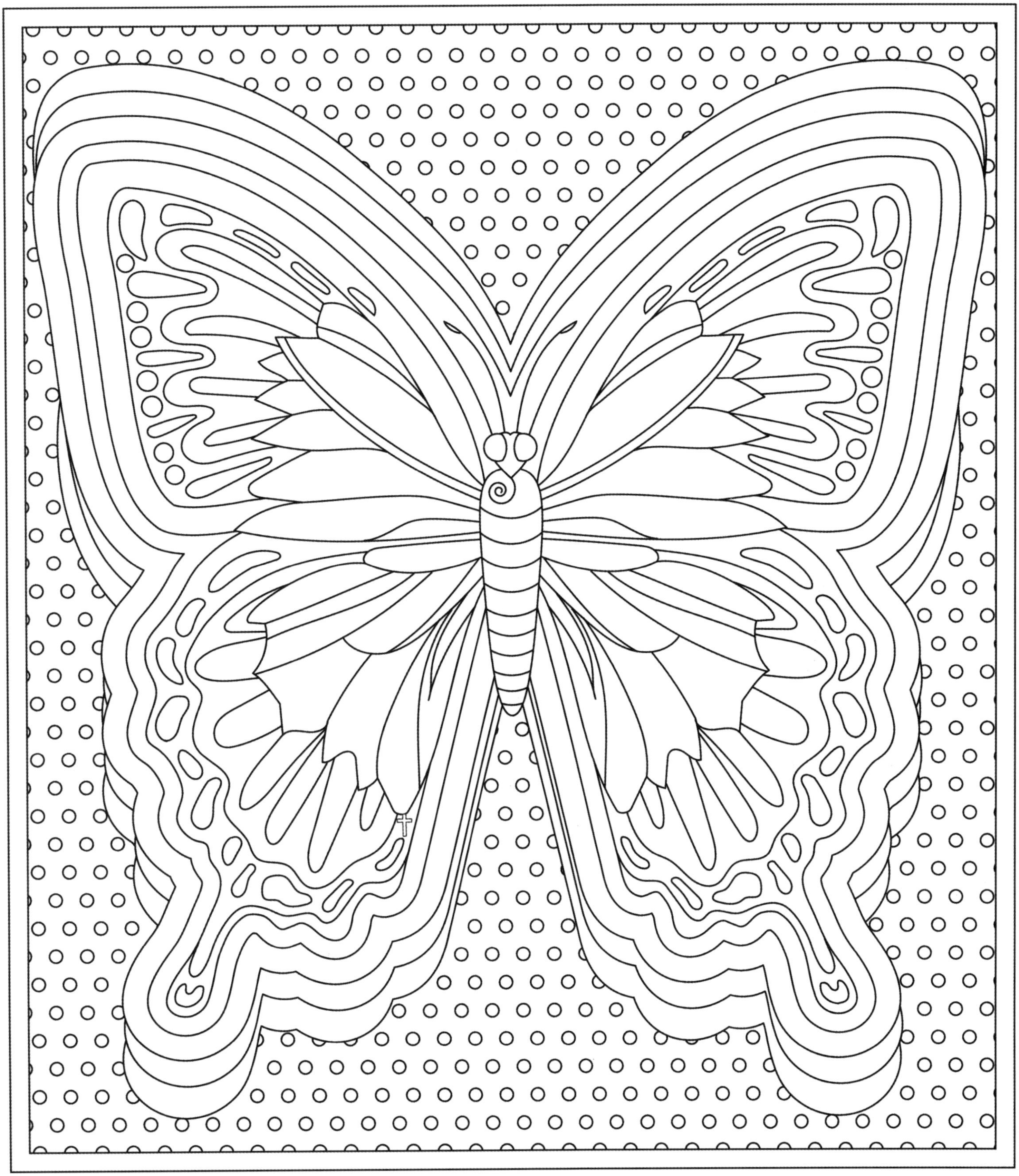

Therefore if any man be in Christ, he is a new creature: old things are passed away; behold, all things are become new.

2 Corinthians 5:17

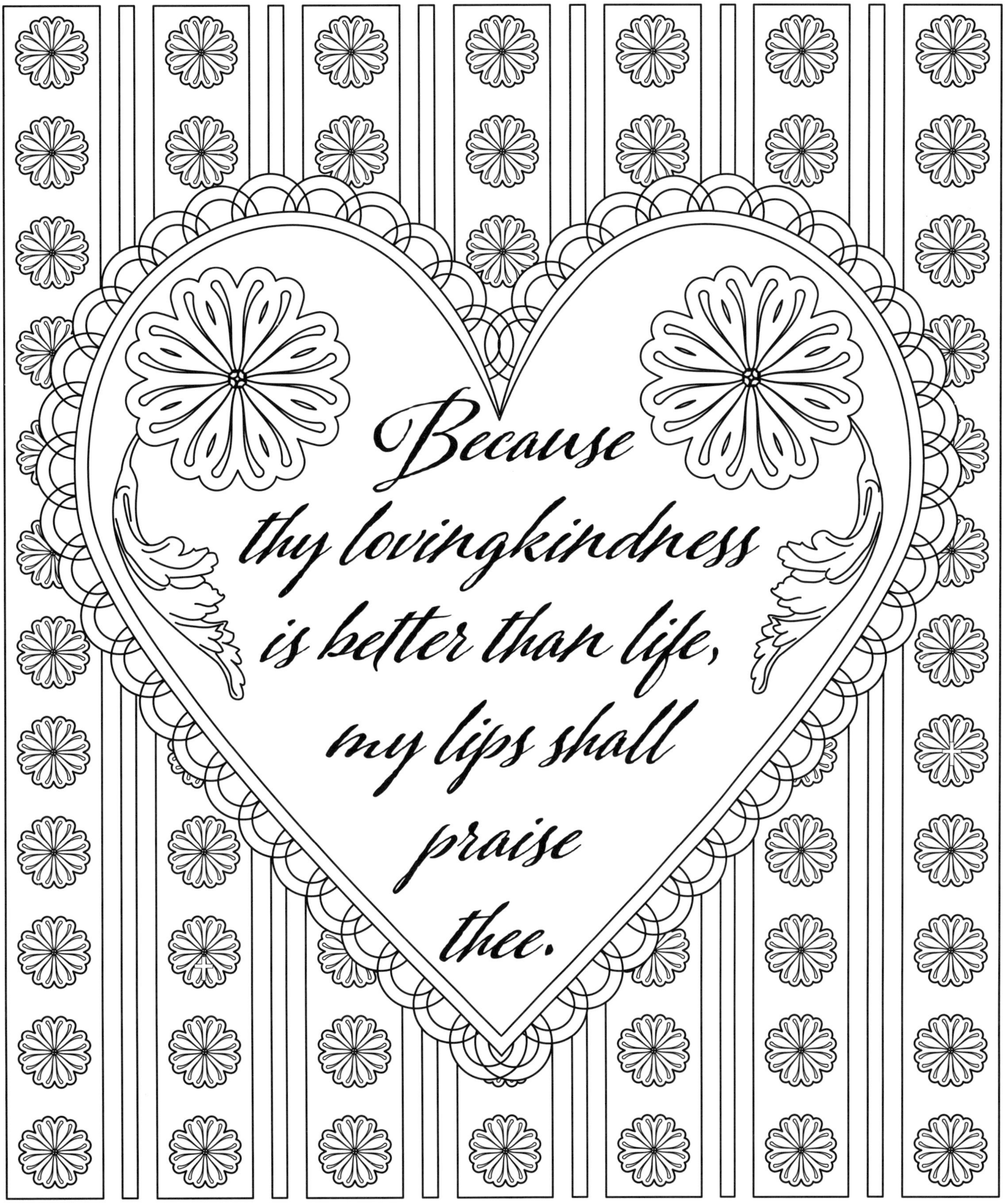

Because thy lovingkindness is better than life, my lips shall praise thee.
Psalm 63:3

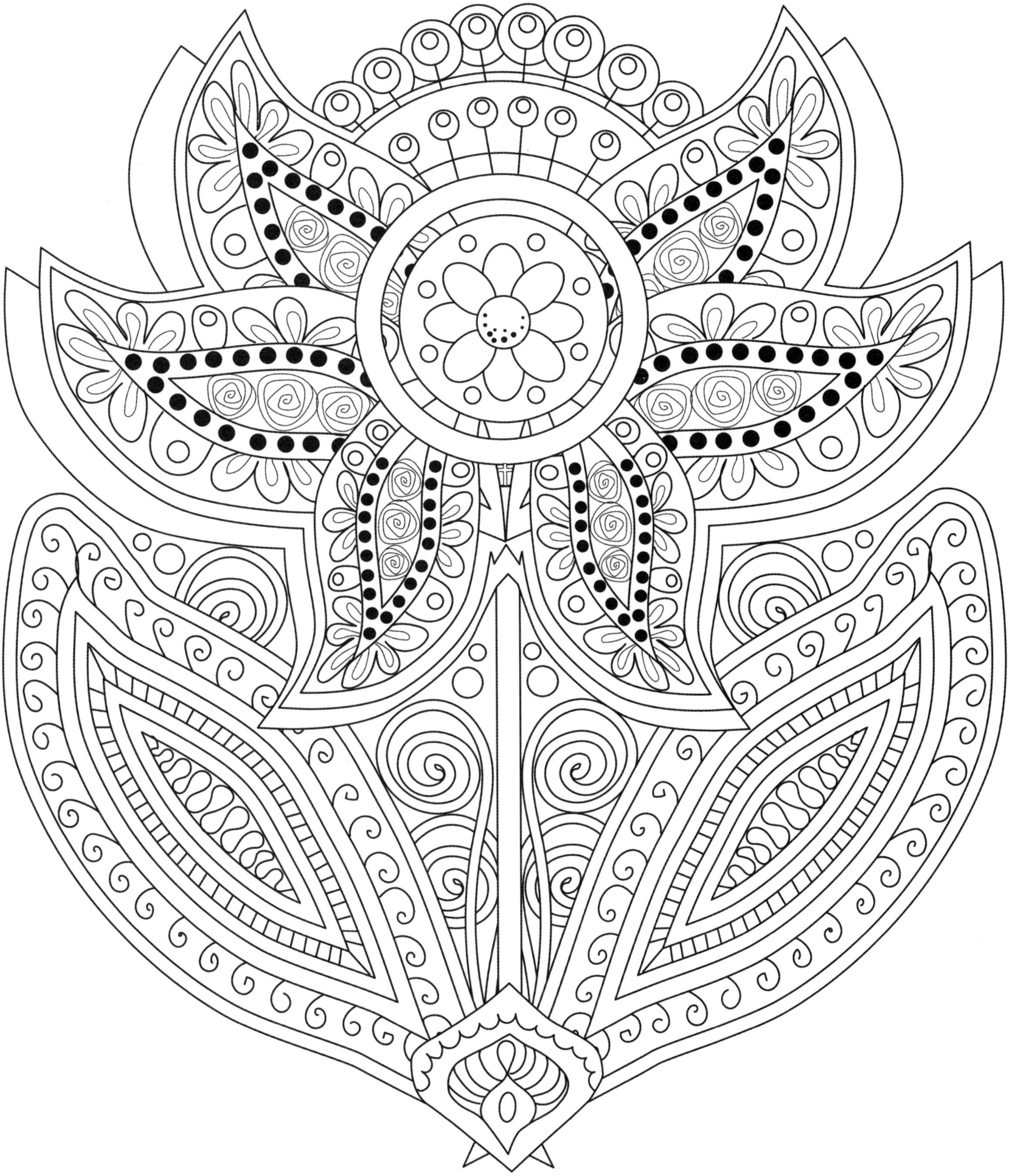

Trust in the LORD with all thine heart;
and lean not unto thine own understanding.
Proverbs 3:5

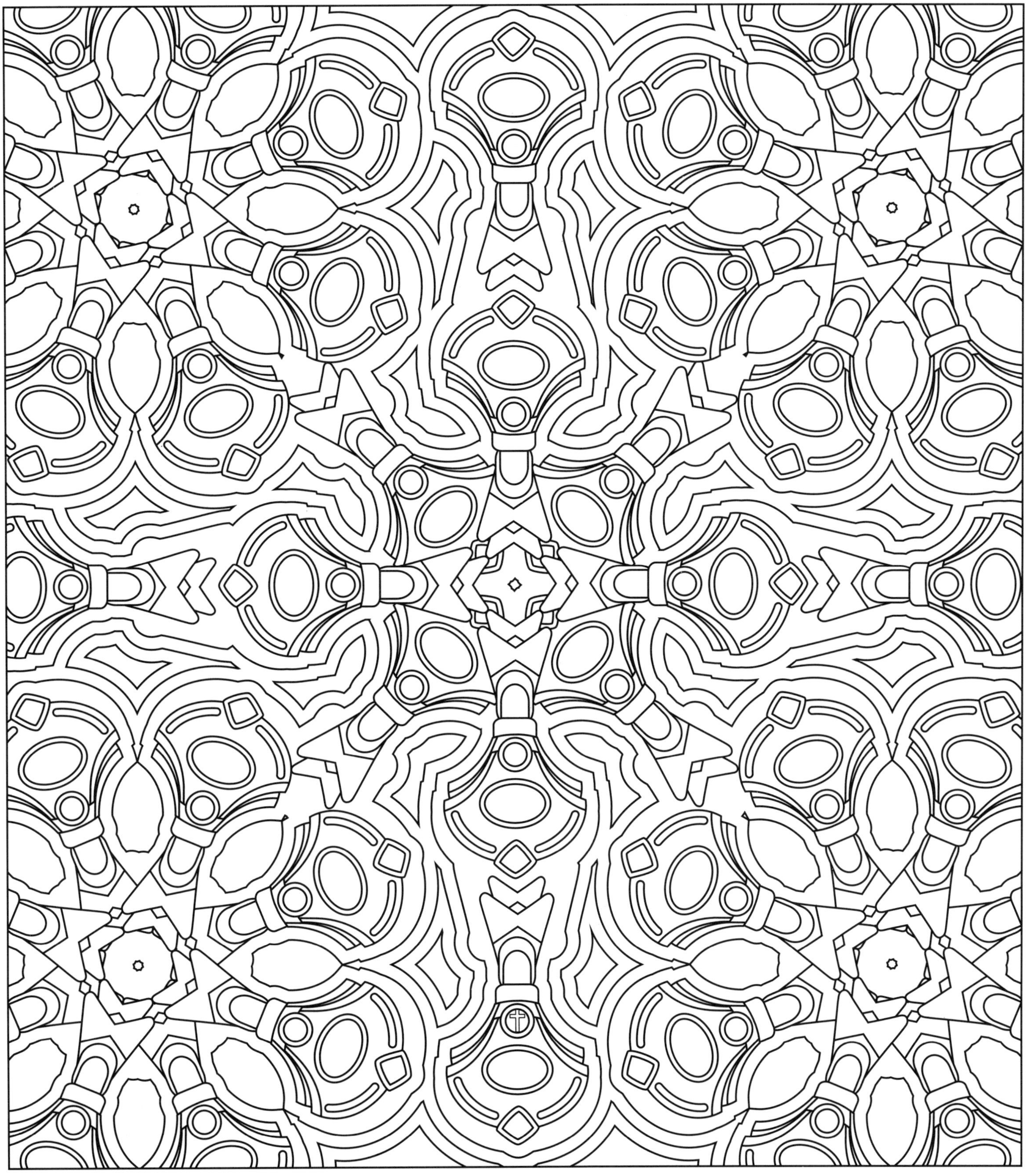

Give thanks unto the LORD, call upon his name,
make known his deeds among the people.
1 Chronicles 16:8

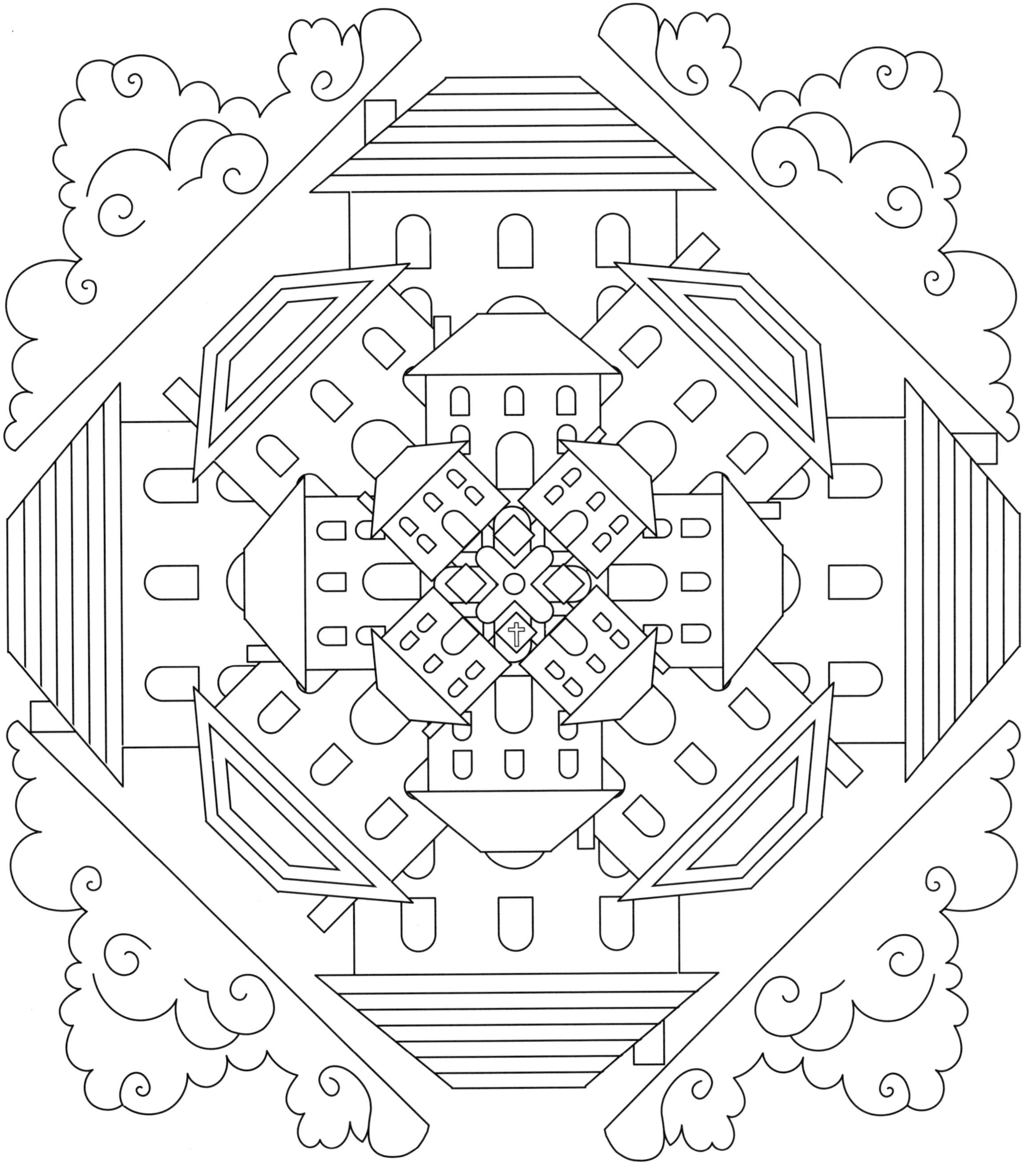

Except the LORD build the house, they labour in vain that build it: except the LORD keep the city, the watchman waketh [but] in vain.

Psalm 127:1

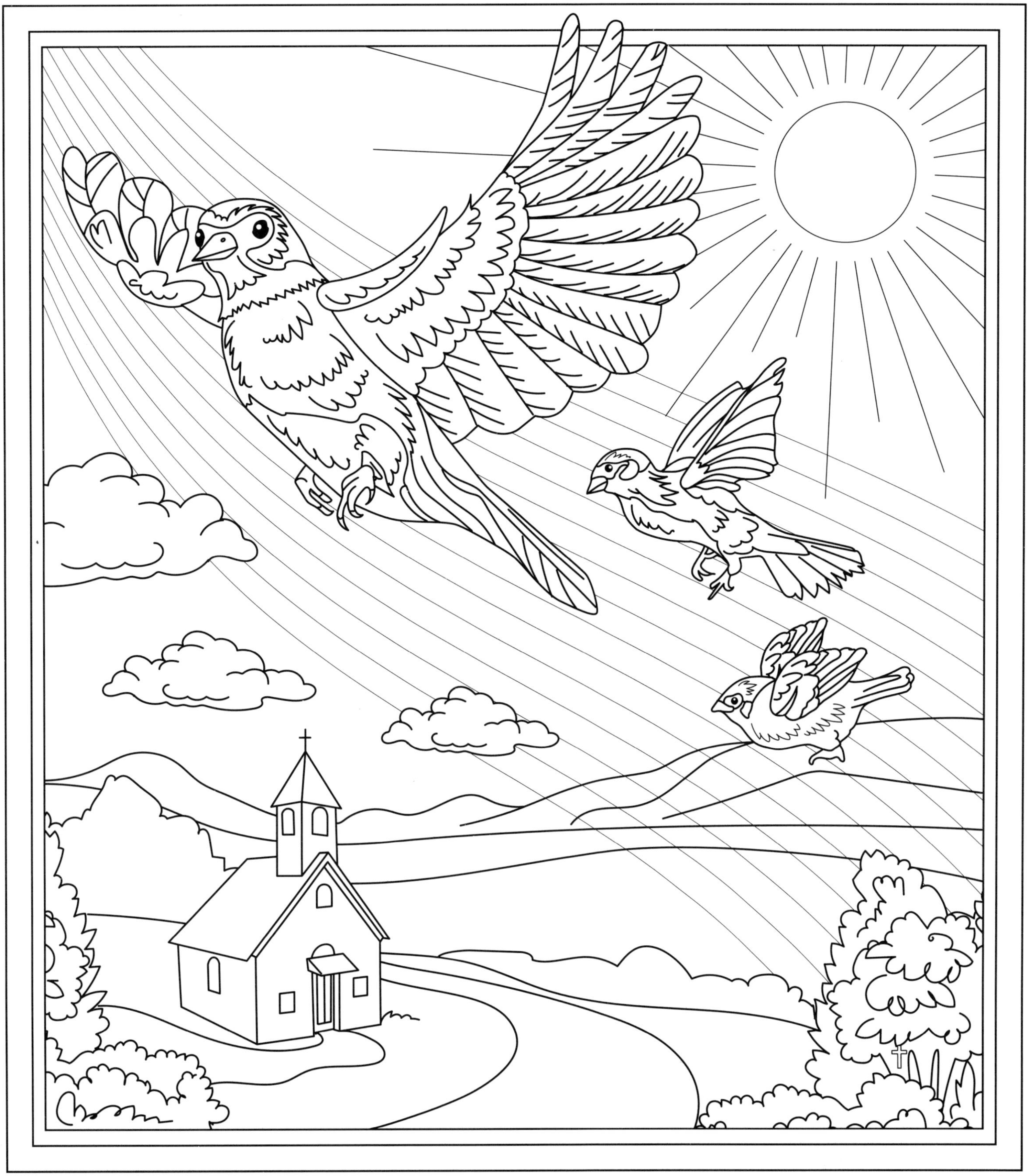

Keep me as the apple of the eye, hide me under the shadow of thy wings.
Psalm 17:8

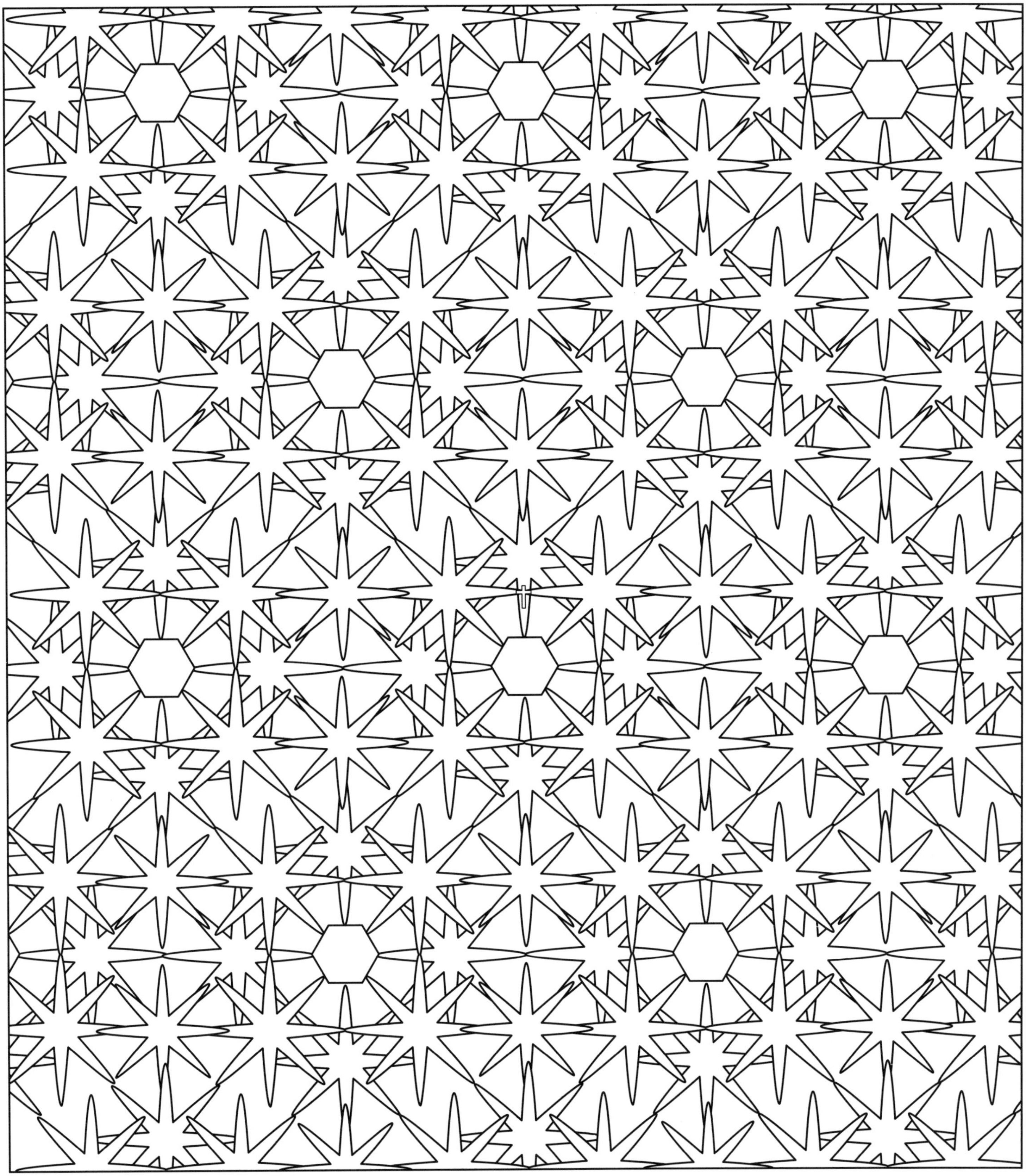

That ye may with one mind [and] one mouth glorify God,
even the Father of our Lord Jesus Christ.

Romans 15:6

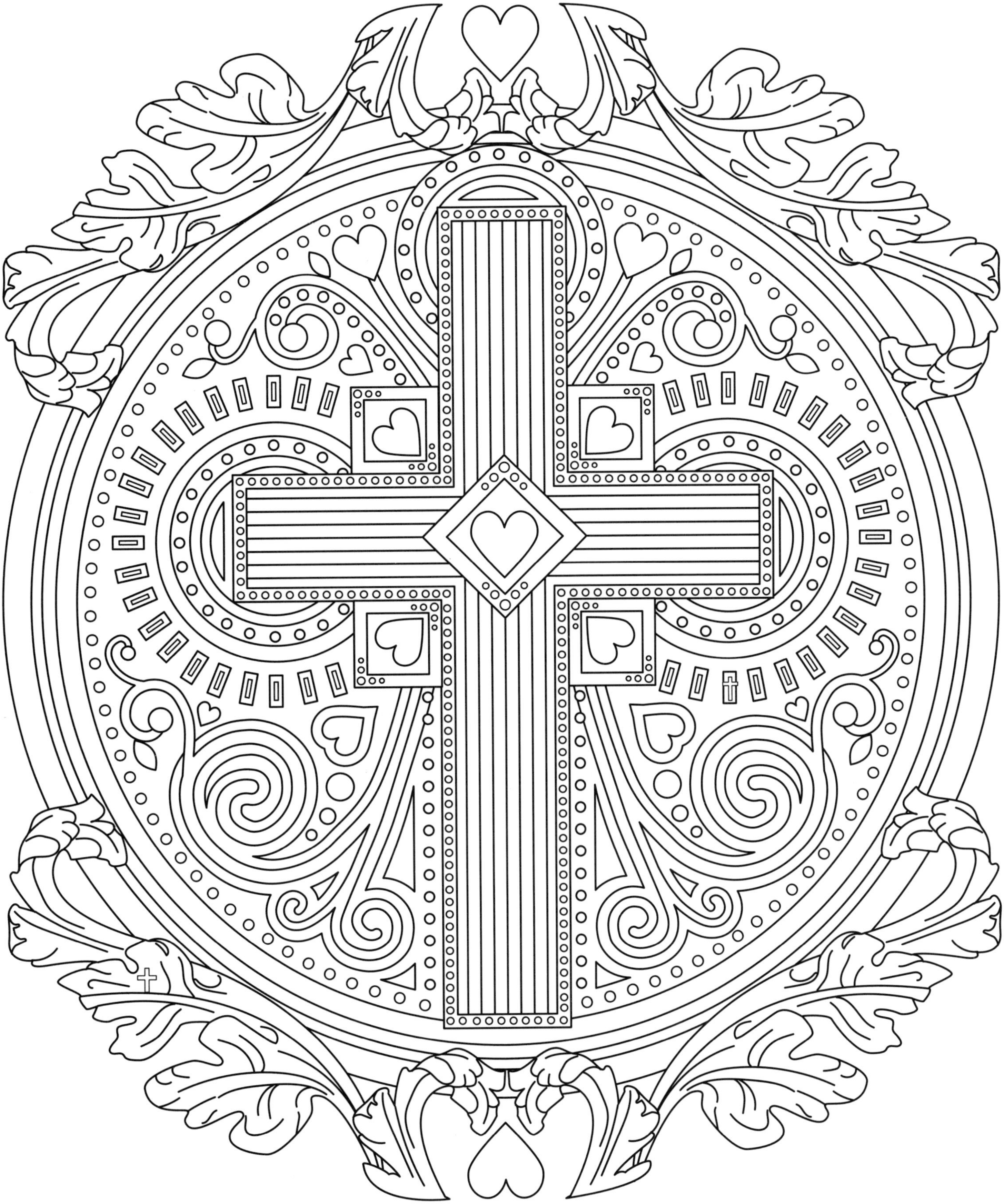

With God all things are possible.
Matthew 19:26

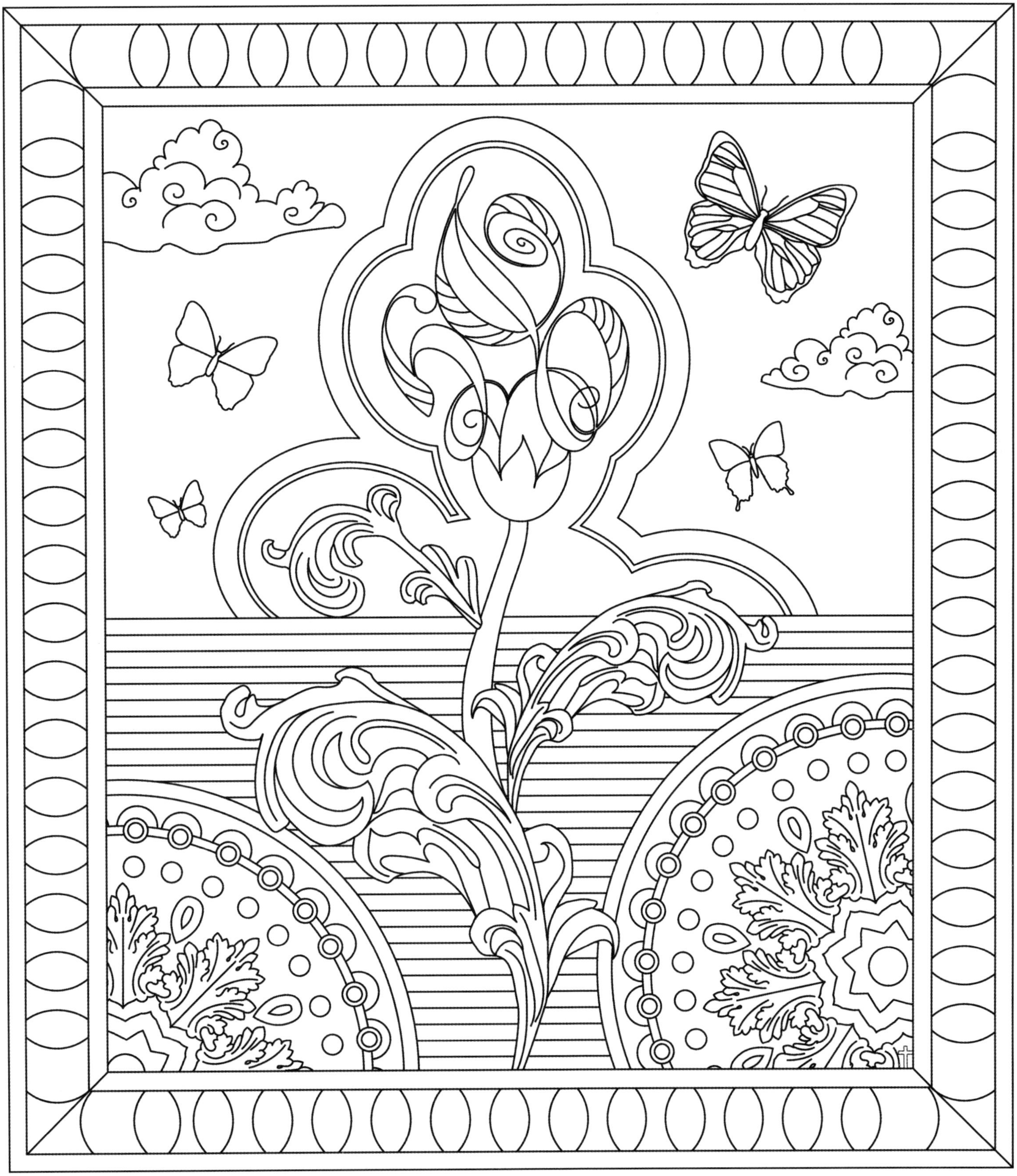

Beloved, if God so loved us, we ought also to love one another.
1 John 4:11

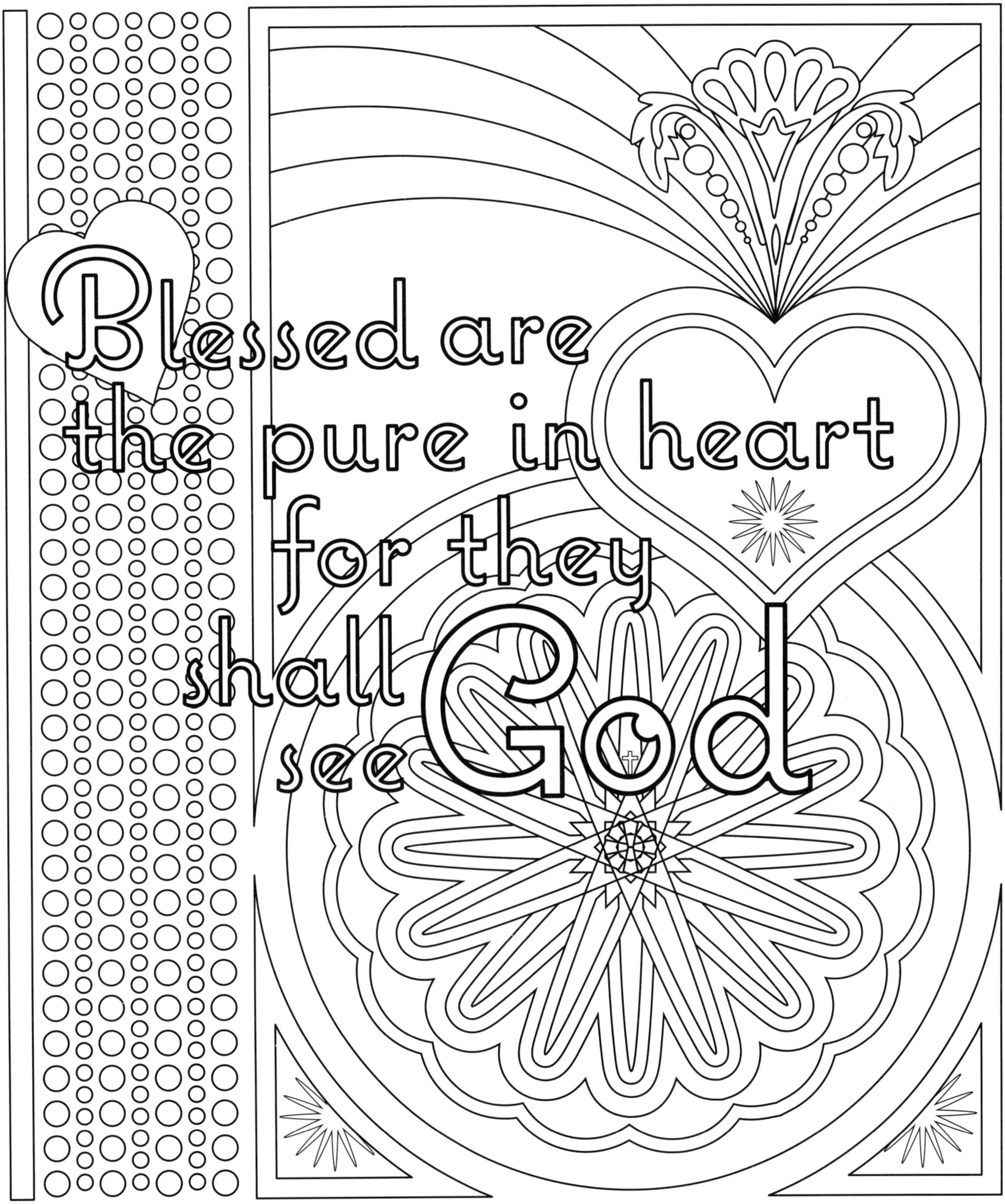

Blessed are the pure in heart: for they shall see God.
Matthew 5:8

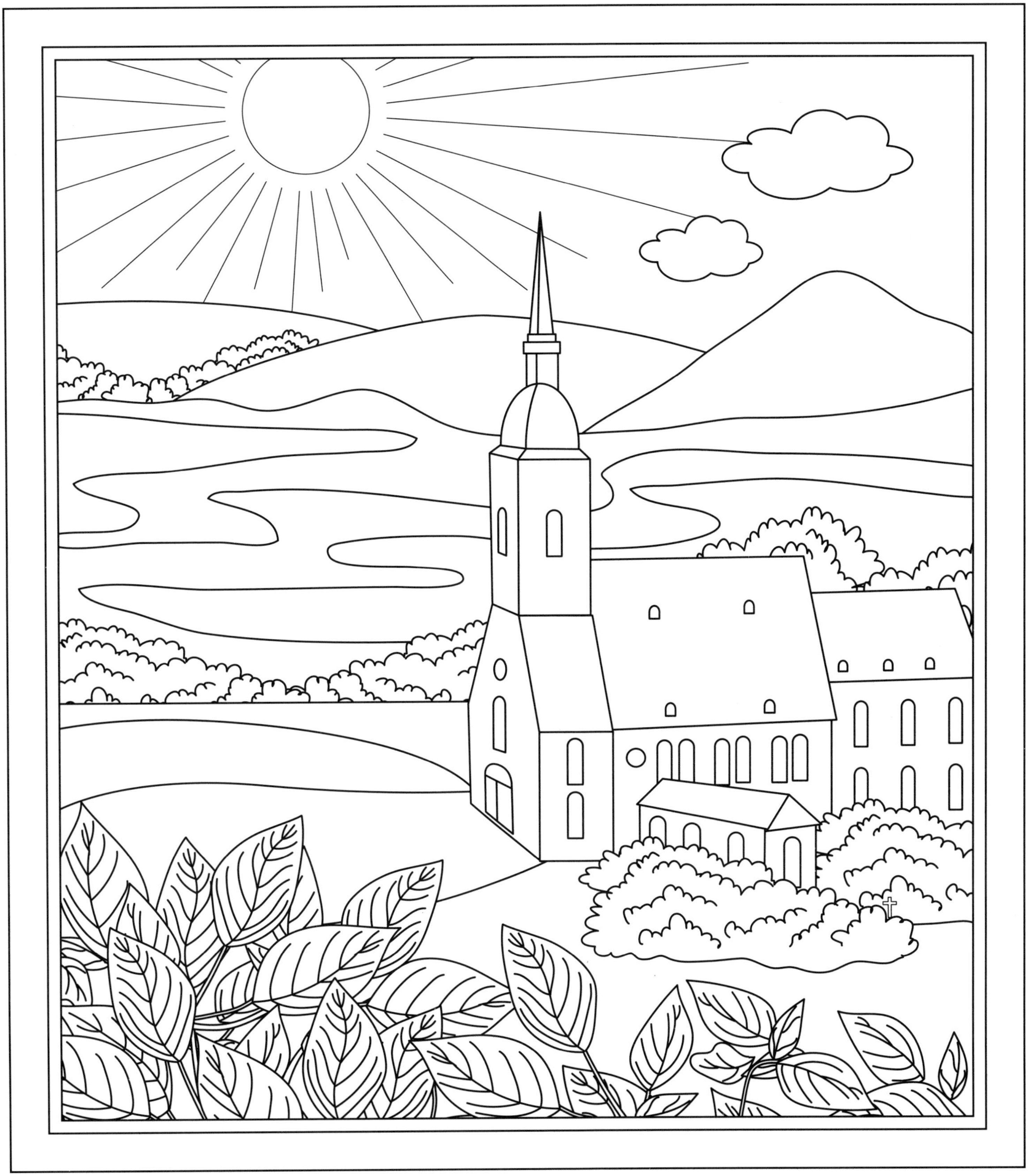

As we have therefore opportunity, let us do good unto all [men], especially unto them who are of the household of faith.

Galatians 6:10

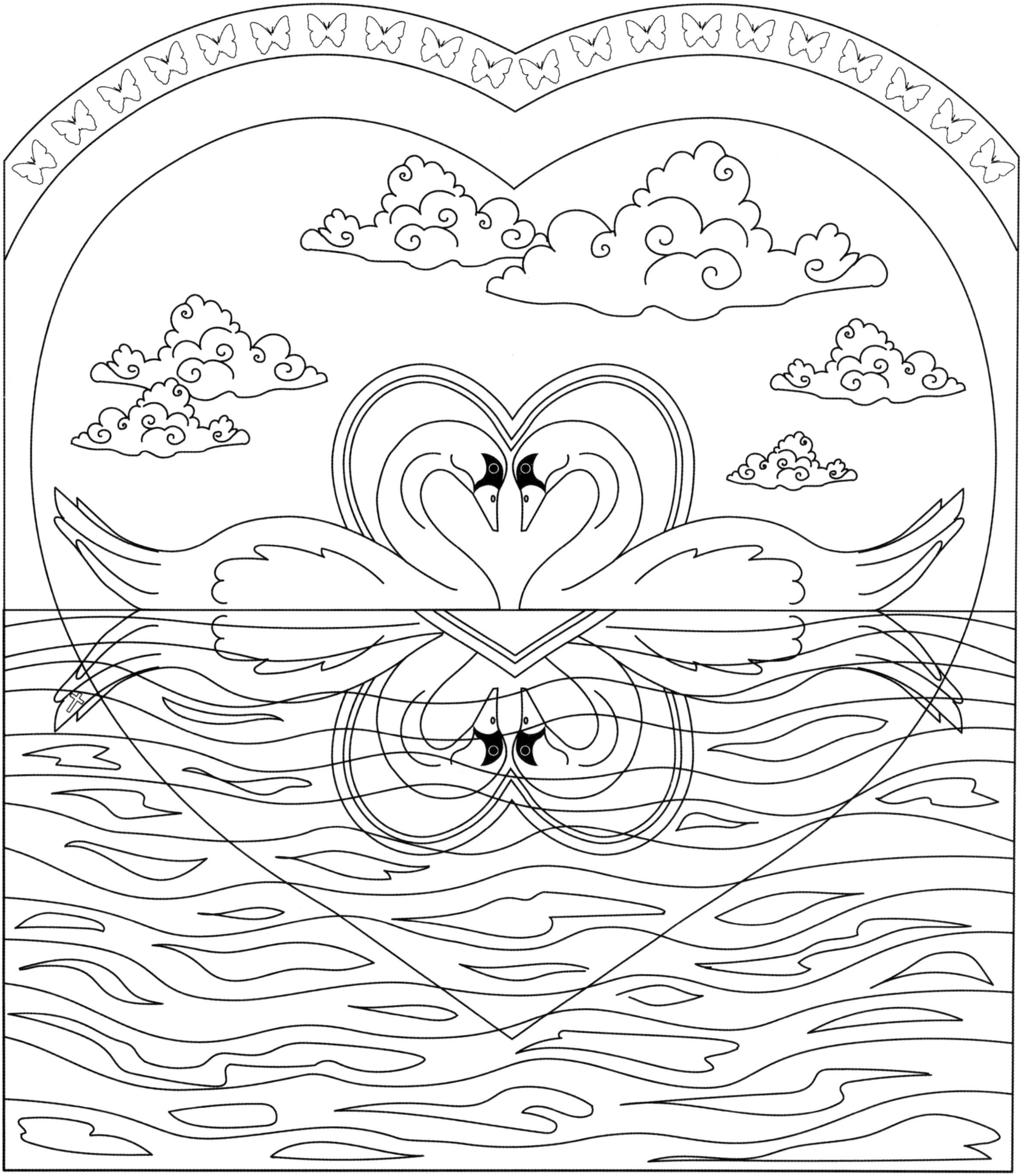

Many waters cannot quench love, neither can the floods drown it.
Song of Solomon 8:7

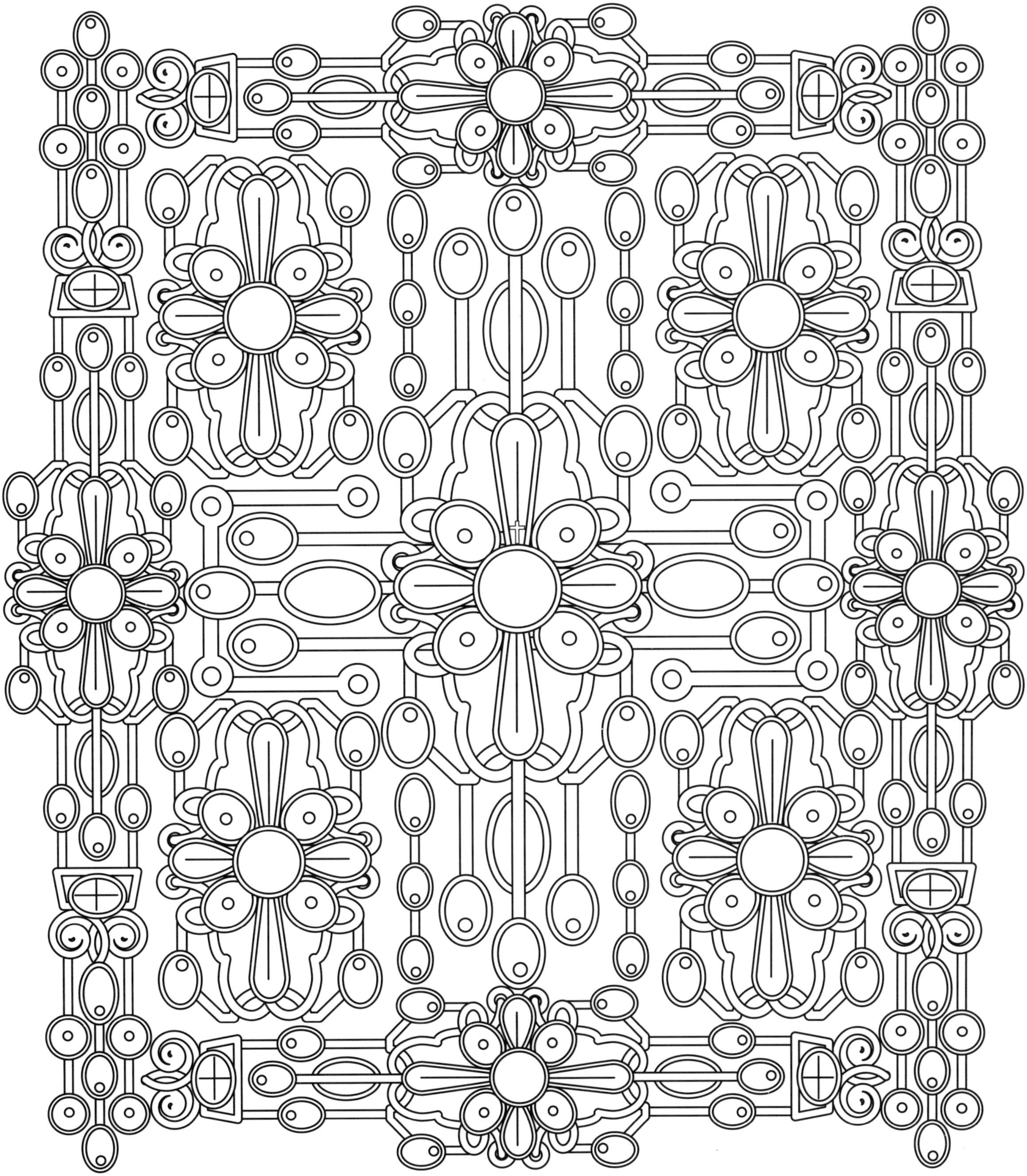

Now faith is the substance of things hoped for, the evidence of things not seen.
Hebrews 11:1

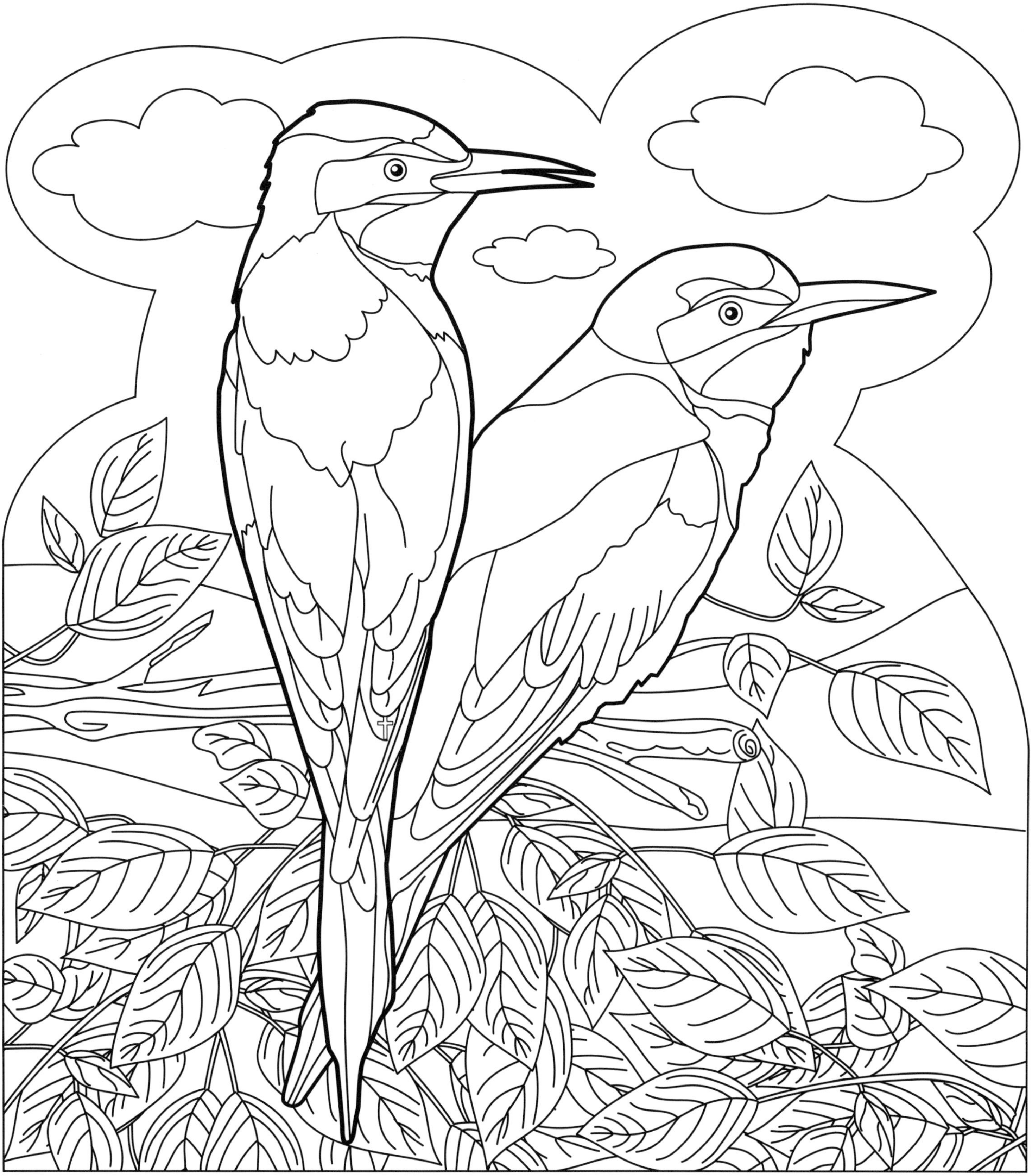

Wherefore comfort yourselves together, and edify one another, even as also ye do.
1 Thessalonians 5:11

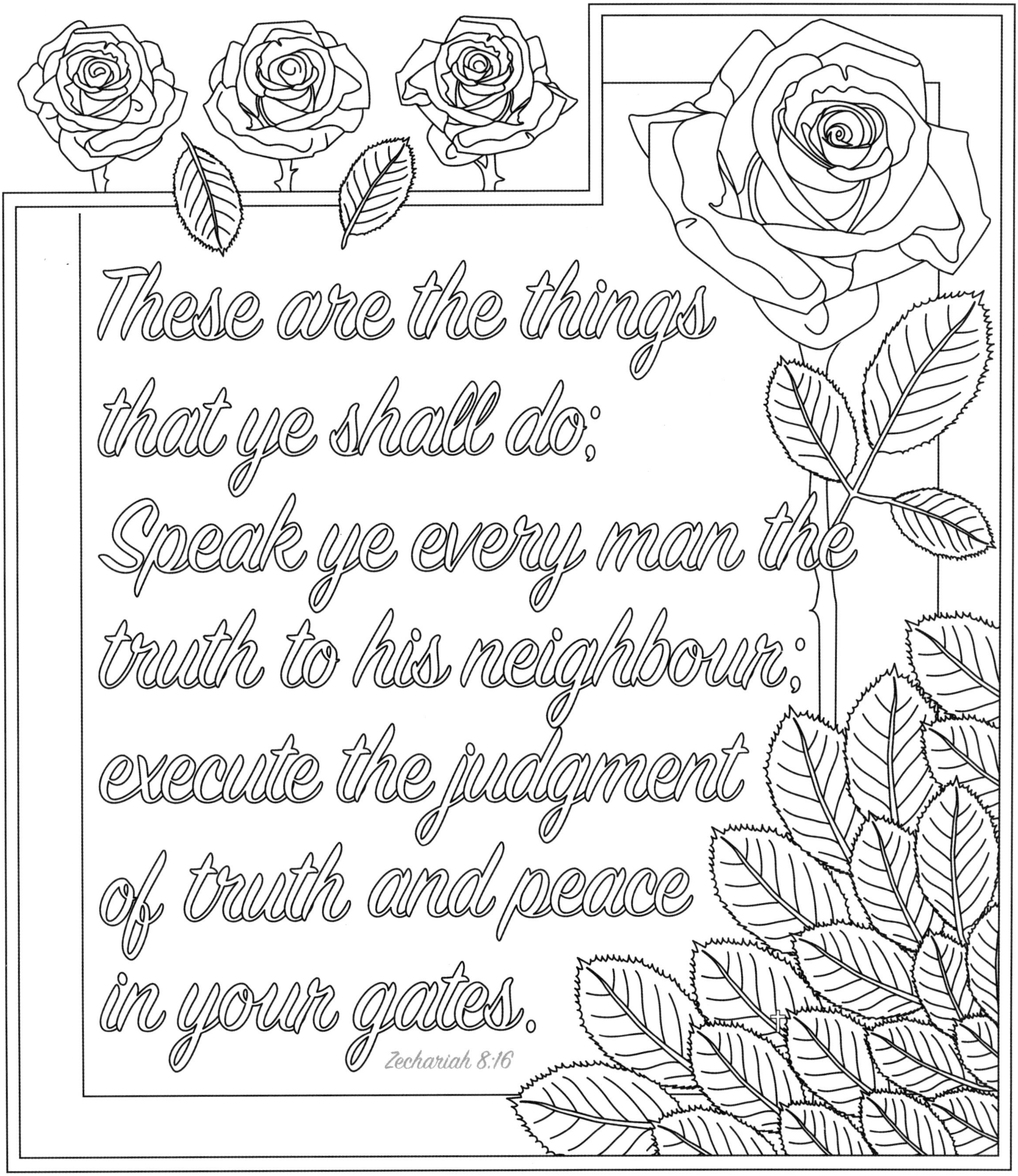

These [are] the things that ye shall do; Speak ye every man the truth to his neighbour; execute the judgment of truth and peace in your gates.
Zechariah 8:16

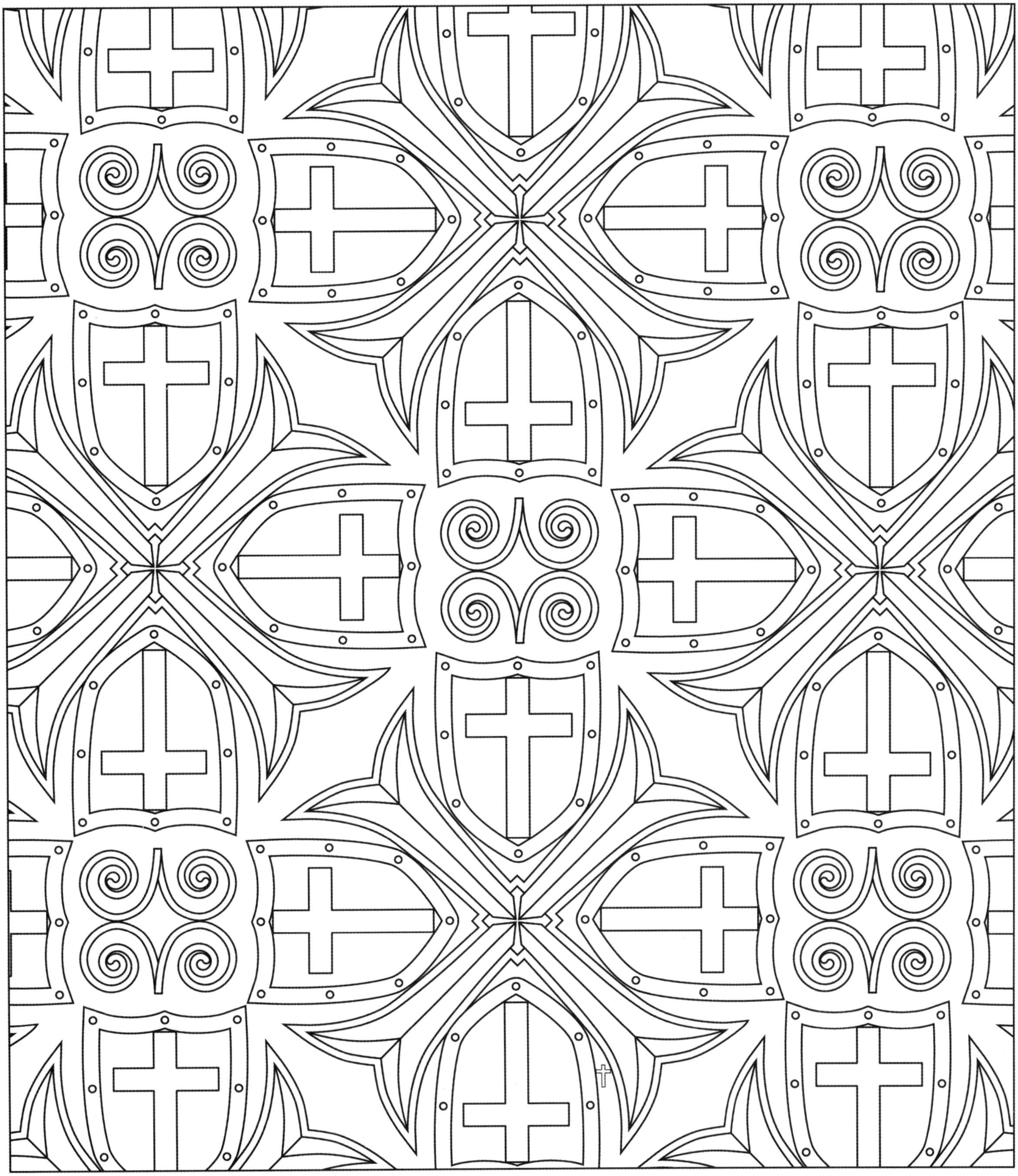

For the LORD your God [is] he that goeth with you, to fight for you against your enemies, to save you.
Deuteronomy 20:4

For God so loved the world, that he gave his only begotten Son, that whosoever believeth in him should not perish, but have everlasting life.

John 3:16

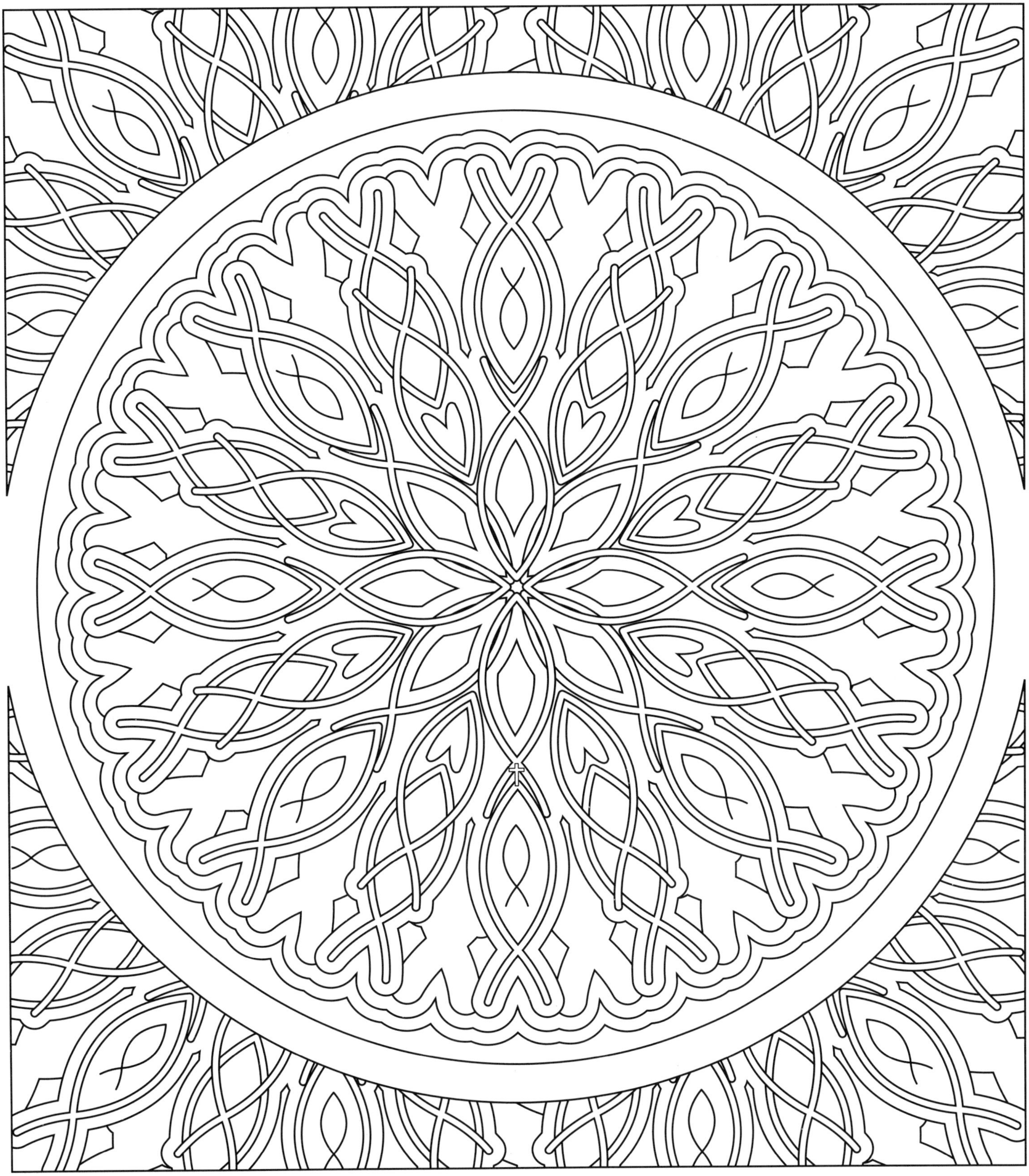

Till we all come in the unity of the faith, and of the knowledge of the Son of God, unto a perfect man, unto the measure of the stature of the fulness of Christ...

Ephesians 4:13

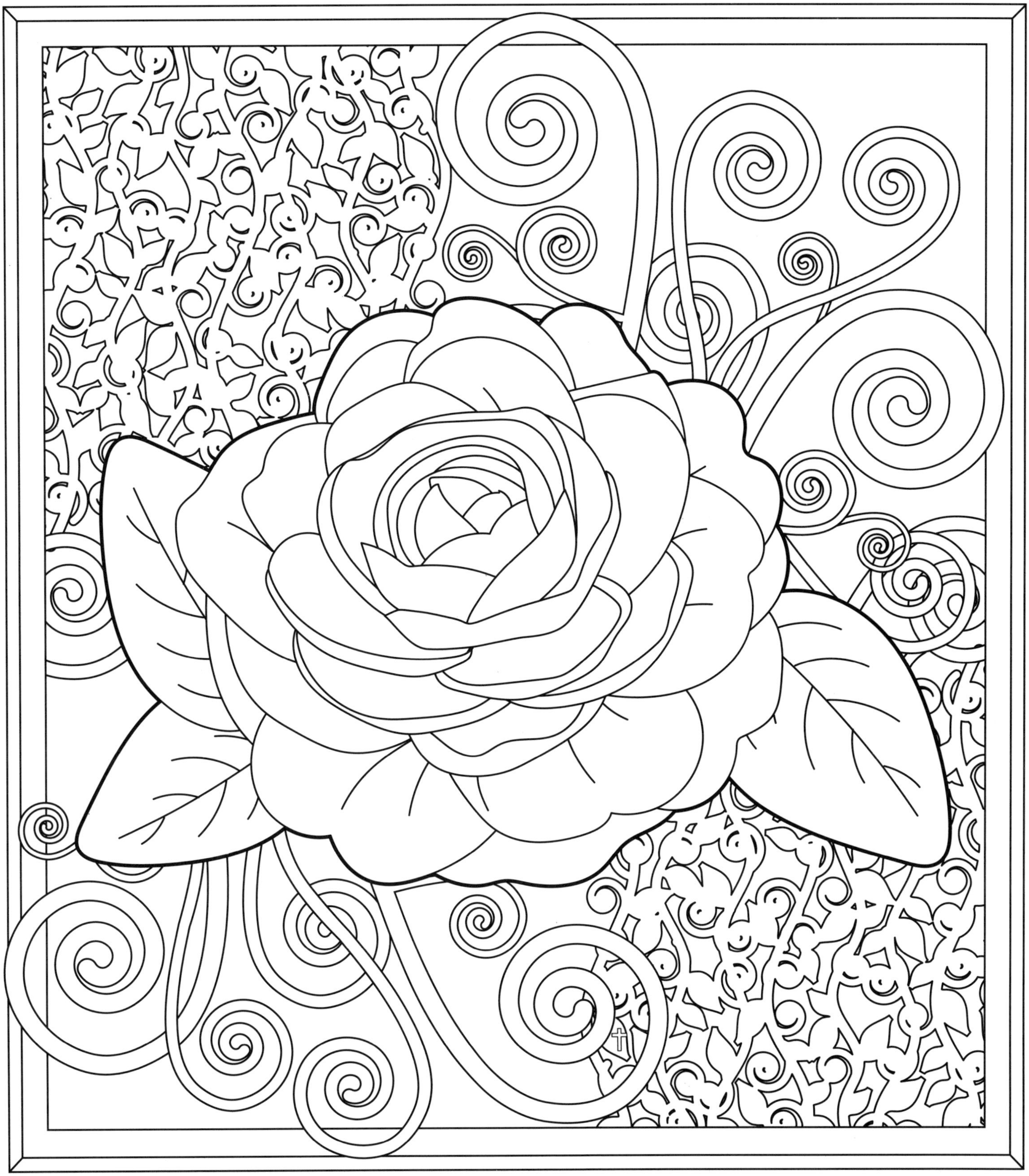

Beloved, I wish above all things that thou mayest prosper and be in health,
even as thy soul prospereth.
3 John 1:2

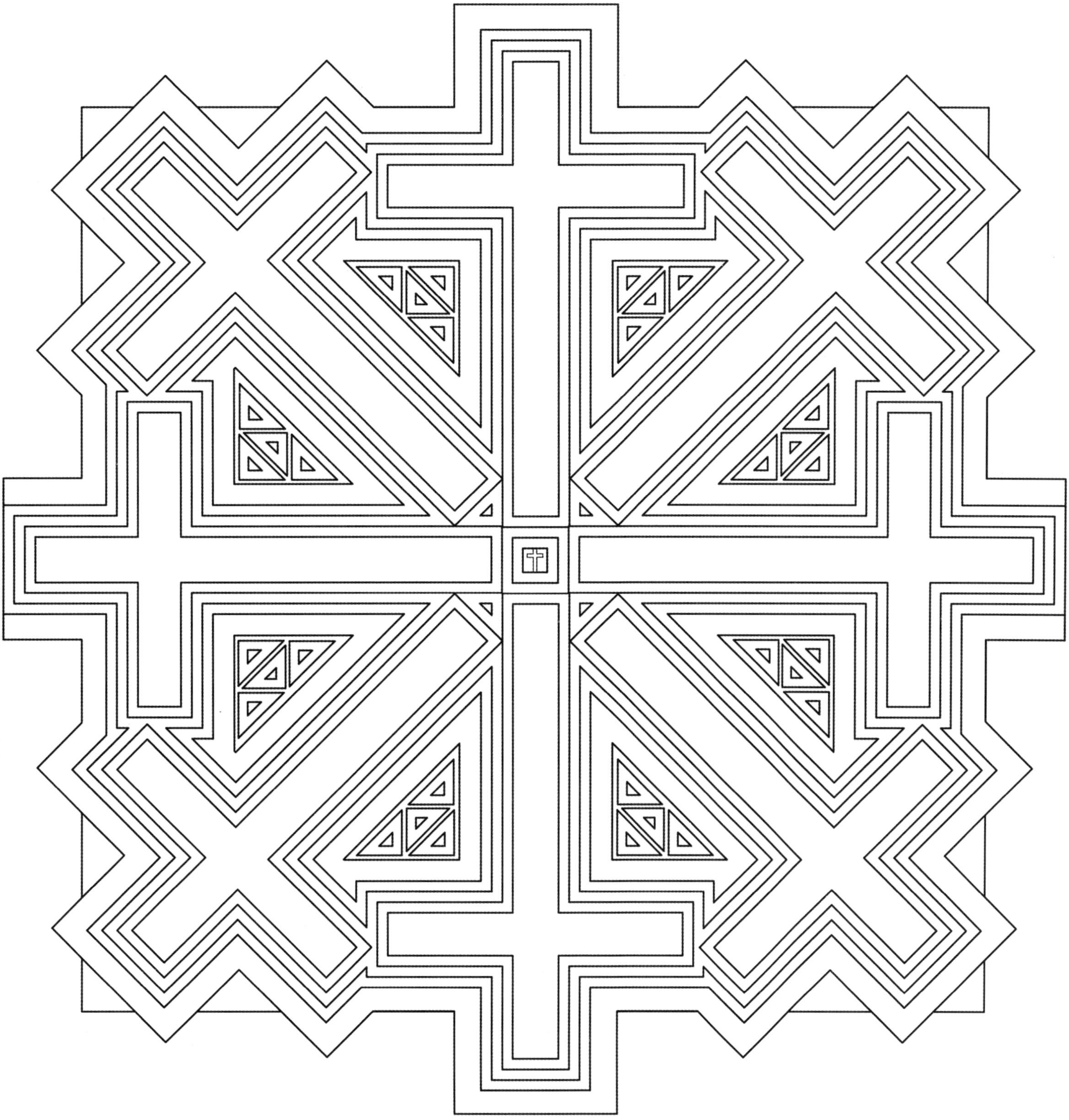

For his merciful kindness is great toward us: and the truth of the LORD endureth for ever. Praise ye the LORD.

Psalm 117:2

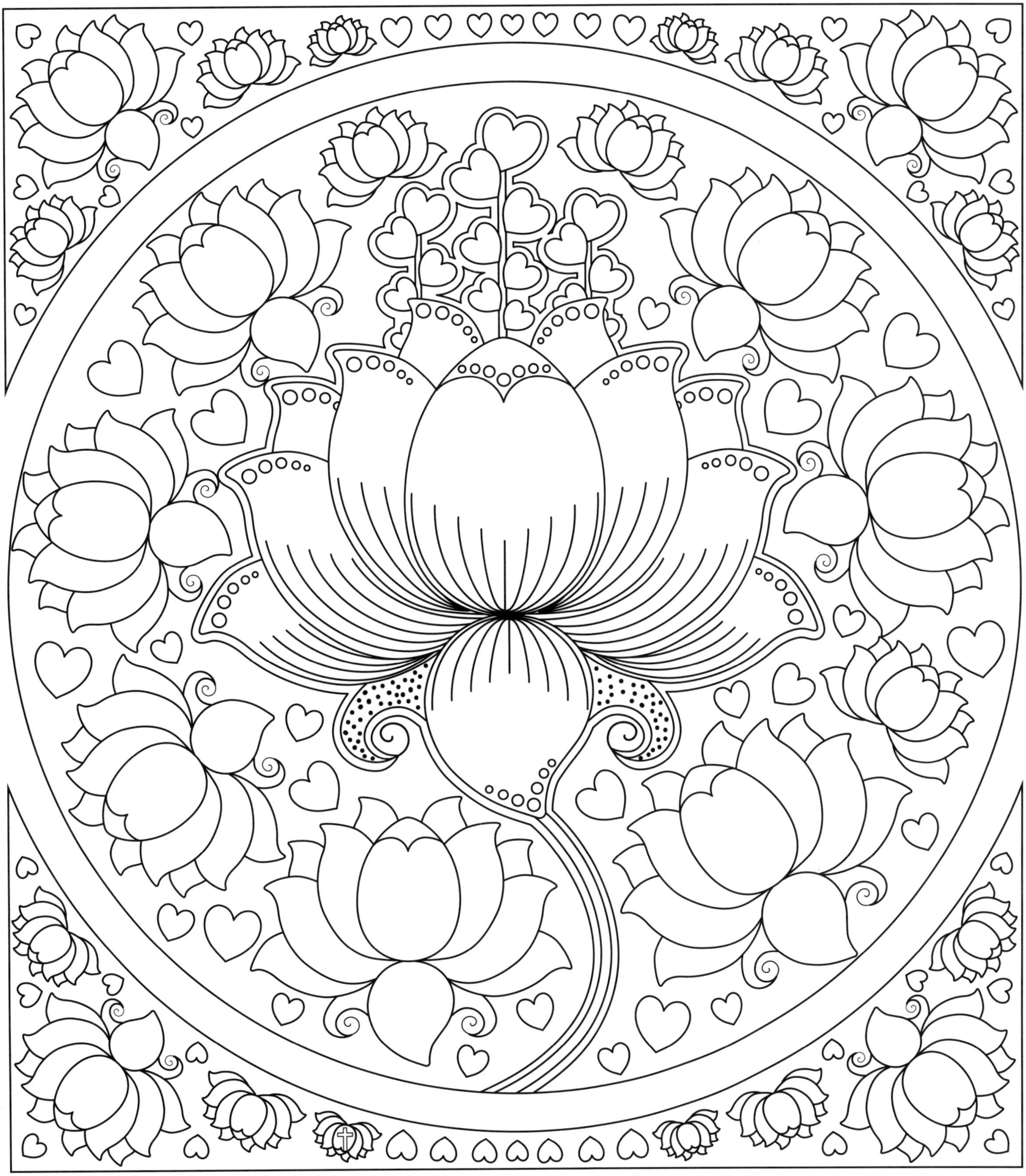

Blessed are the merciful: for they shall obtain mercy.
Matthew 5:7

A merry heart doeth good [like] a medicine:
but a broken spirit drieth the bones.
Proverbs 17:22

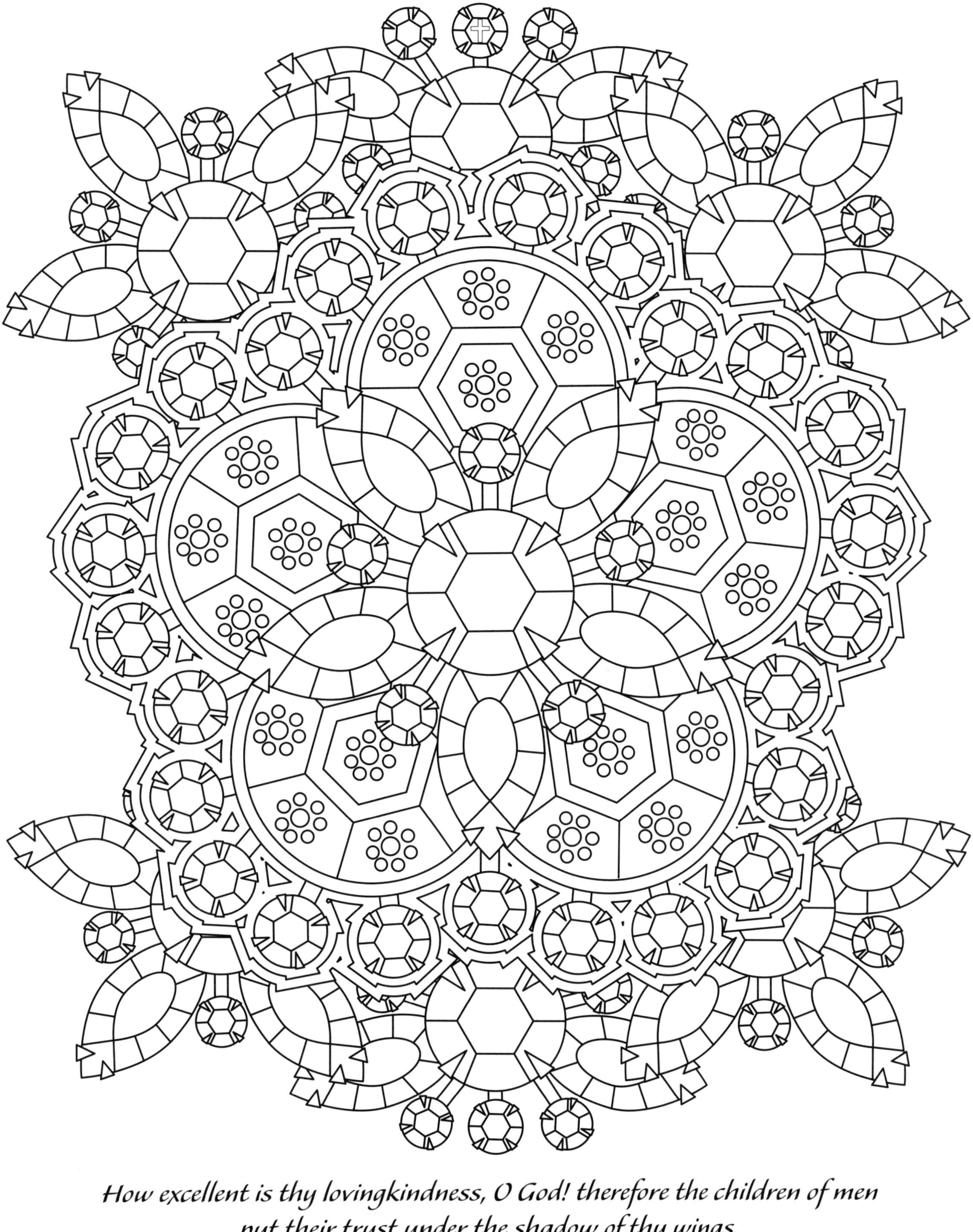

How excellent is thy lovingkindness, O God! therefore the children of men put their trust under the shadow of thy wings.

Psalm 36:7

Let us therefore follow after the things which make for peace,
and things wherewith one may edify another.
Romans 14:19

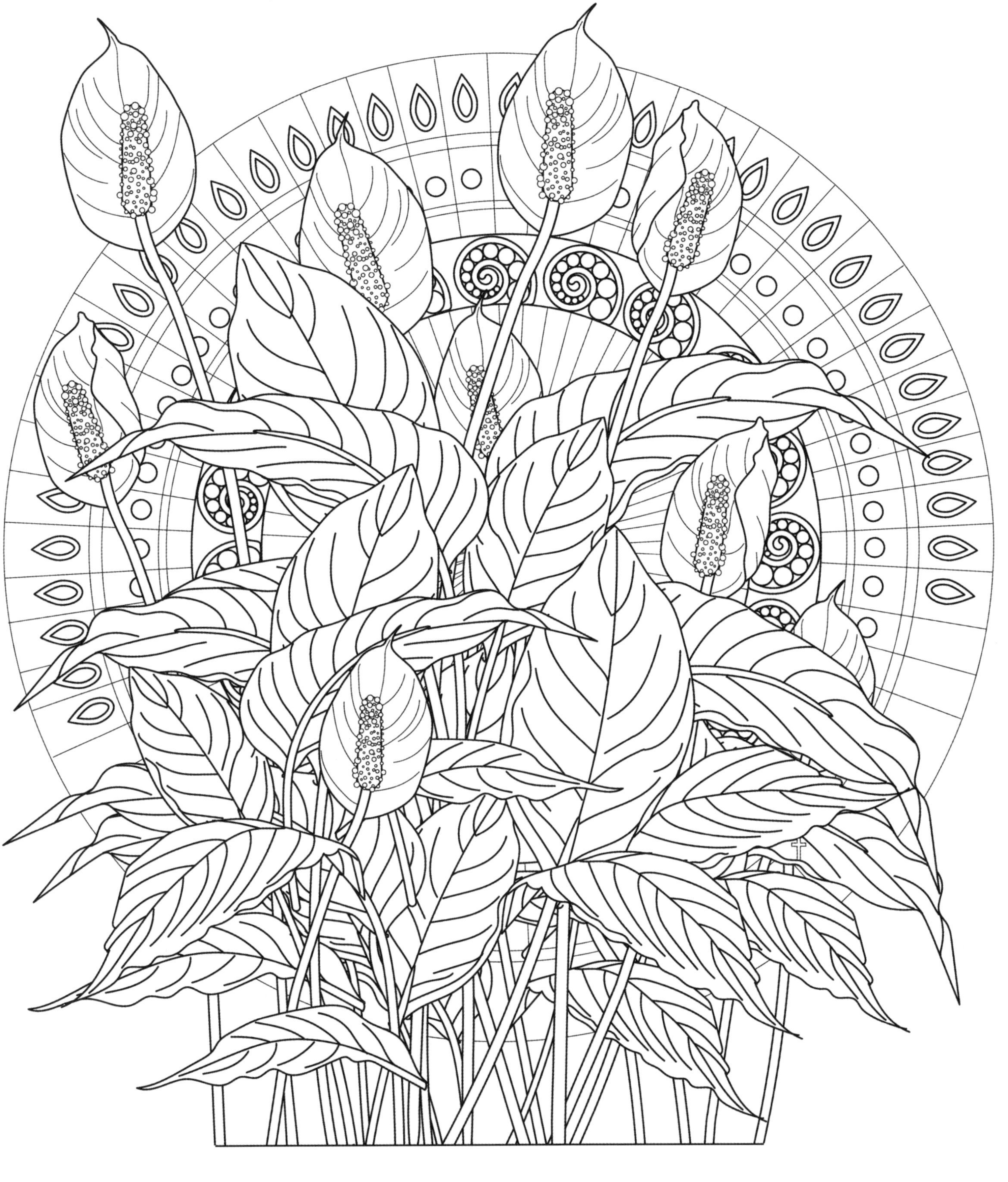

Now the Lord of peace himself give you peace always by all means.
The Lord [be] with you all.
2 Thessalonians 3:16

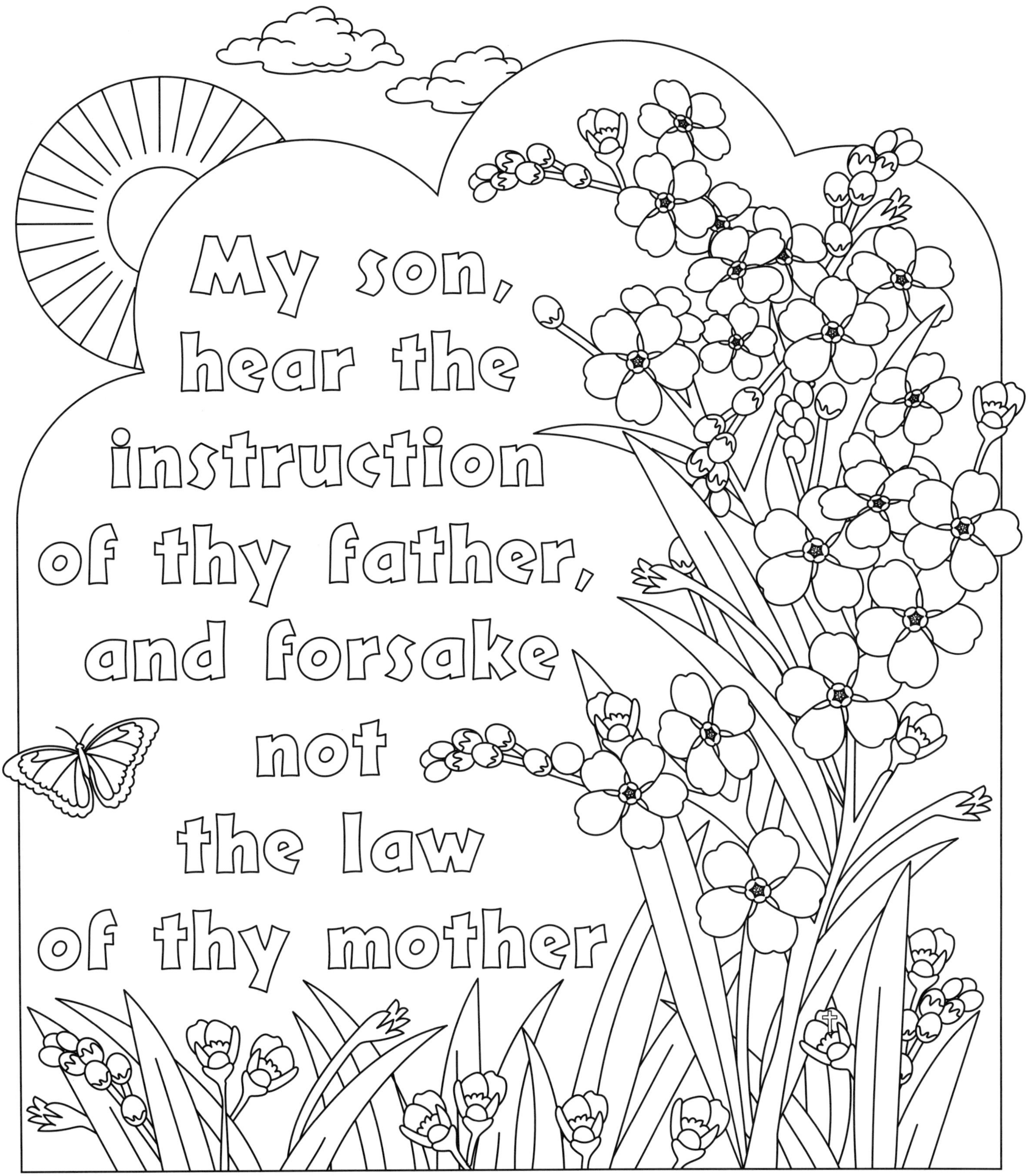

My son, hear the instruction of thy father, and forsake not the law of thy mother.
Proverbs 1:8

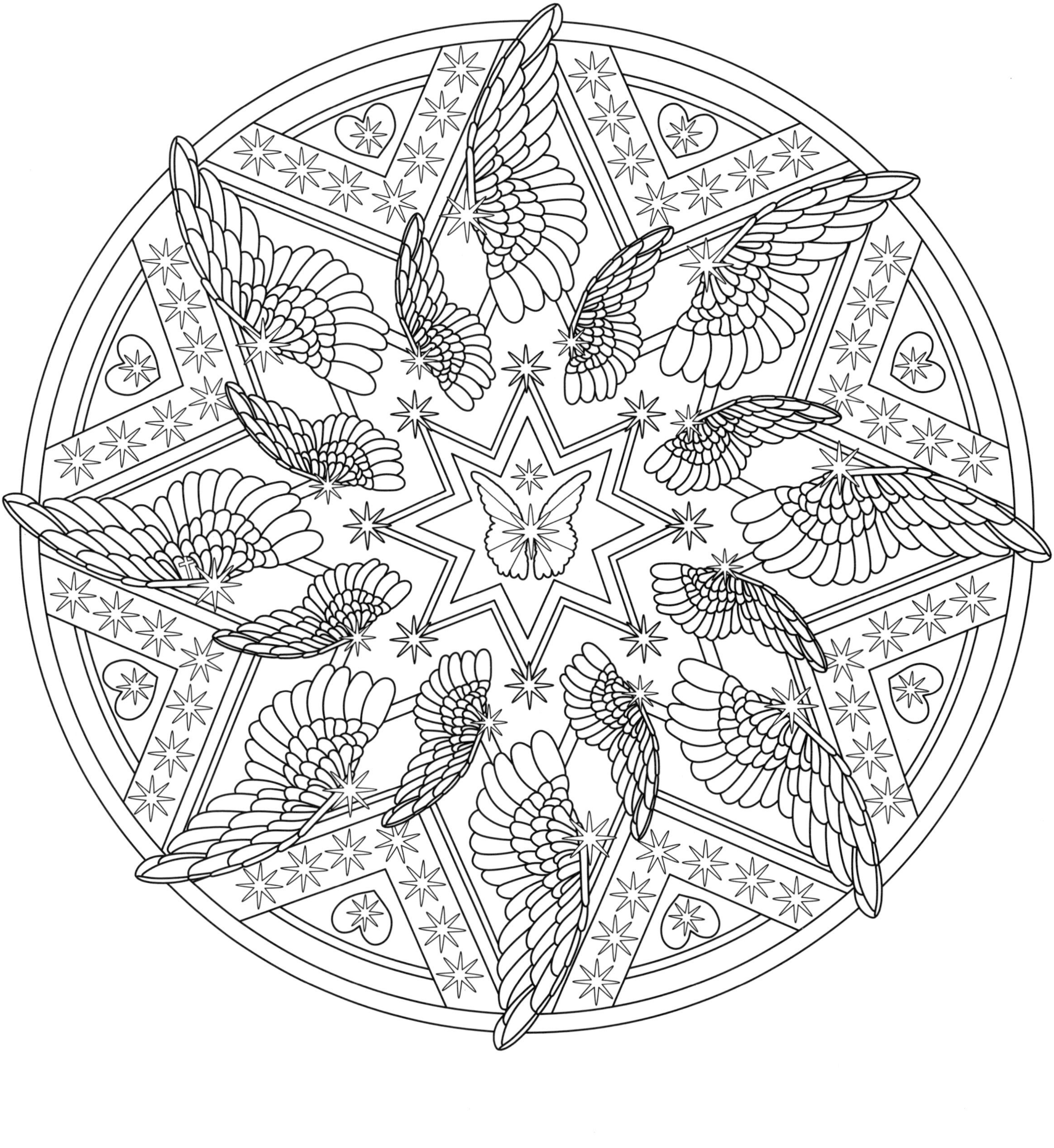

Be not forgetful to entertain strangers:
for thereby some have entertained angels unawares.
Hebrews 13:2

And all thy children [shall be] taught of the LORD;
and great [shall be] the peace of thy children.
Isaiah 54:13

And the multitude of them that believed were of one heart and of one soul.

Acts 4:32

So ought men to love their wives as their own bodies.
He that loveth his wife loveth himself.
Ephesians 5:28

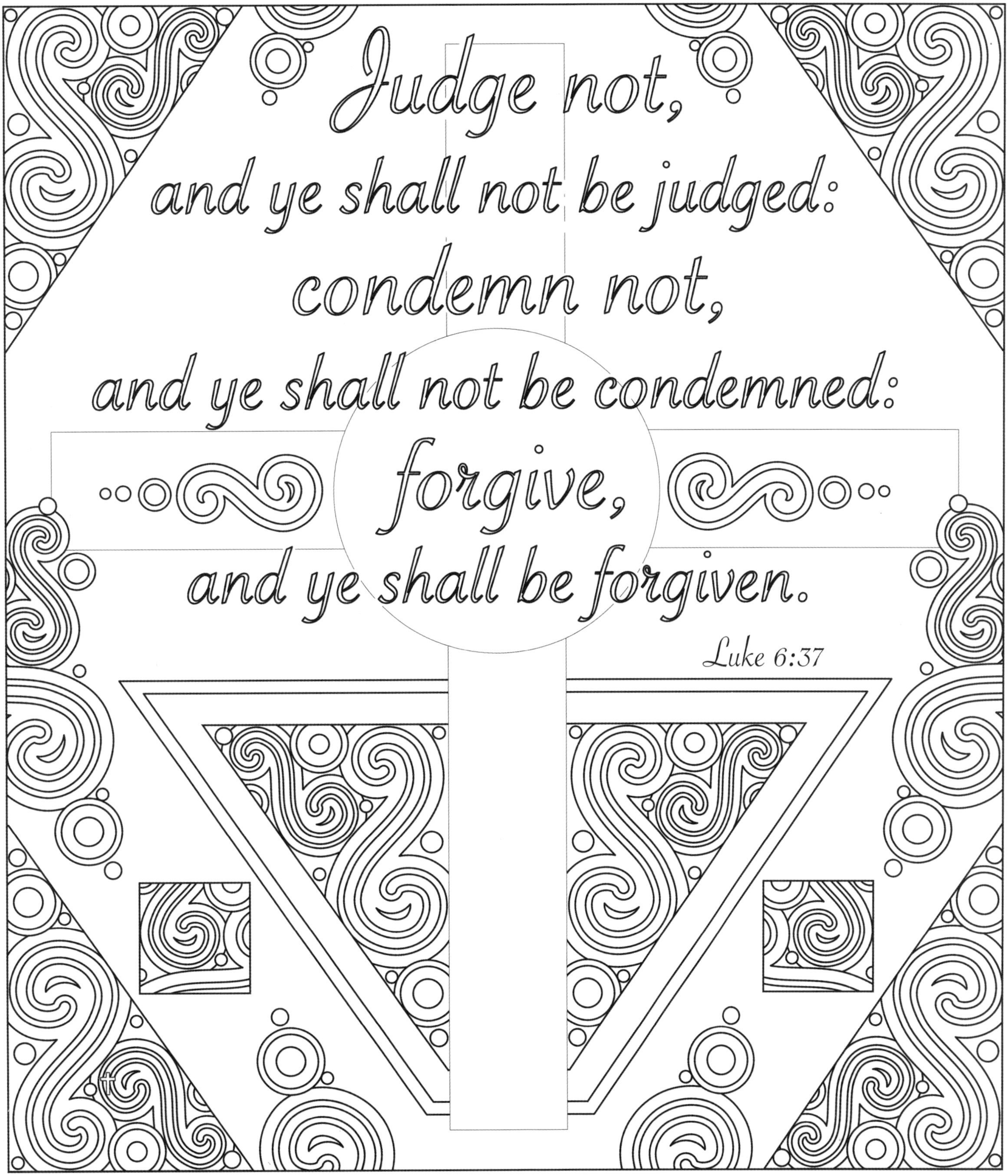

Judge not, and ye shall not be judged: condemn not, and ye shall not be condemned: forgive, and ye shall be forgiven.

Luke 6:37

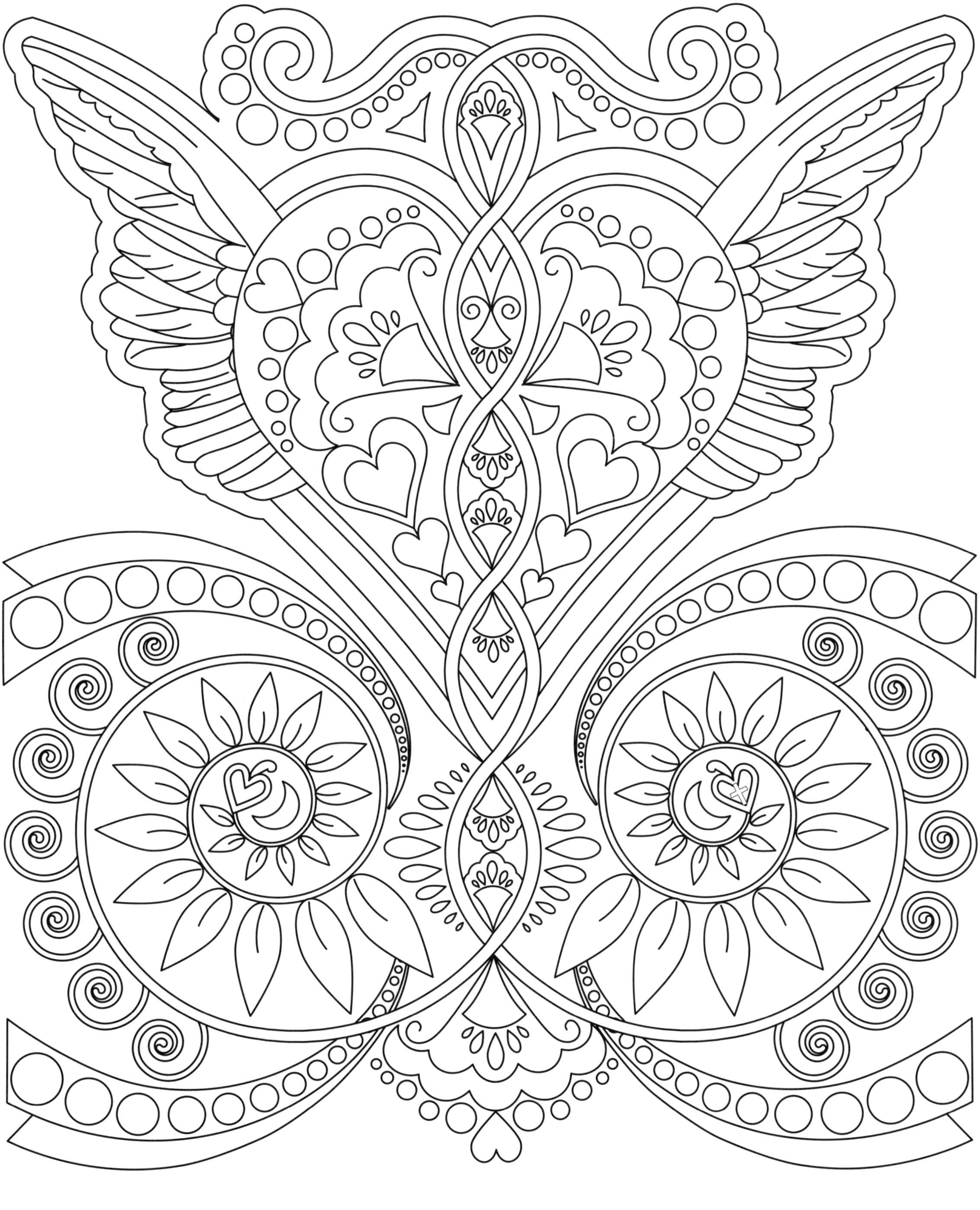

God is love; and he that dwelleth in love dwelleth in God, and God in him.
1 John 4:16

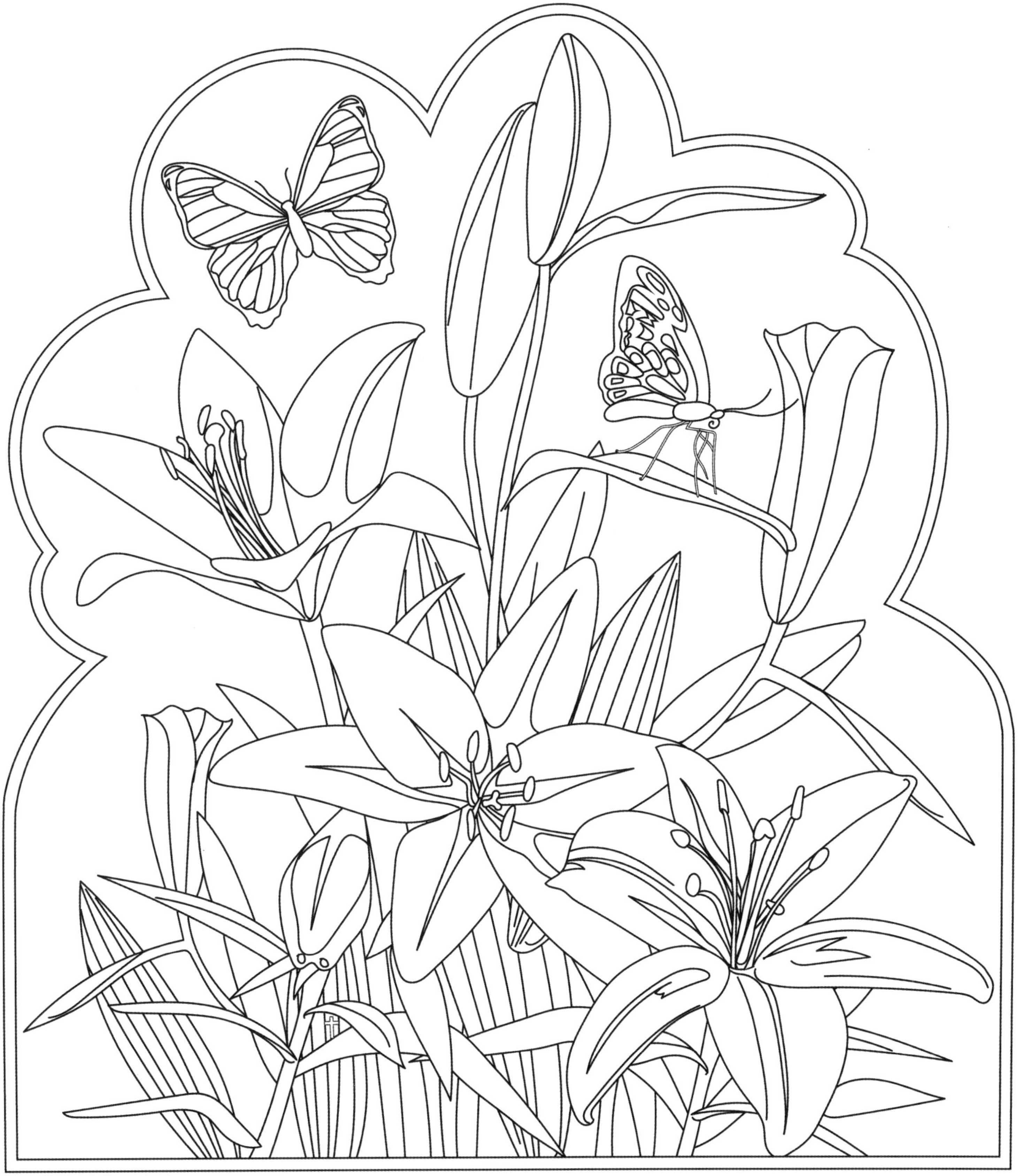

Consider the lilies how they grow: they toil not, they spin not; and yet I say unto you, that Solomon in all his glory was not arrayed like one of these.

Luke 12:27

And the LORD, he it is that doth go before thee; he will be with thee,
he will not fail thee, neither forsake thee: fear not, neither be dismayed.
Deuteronomy 31:8

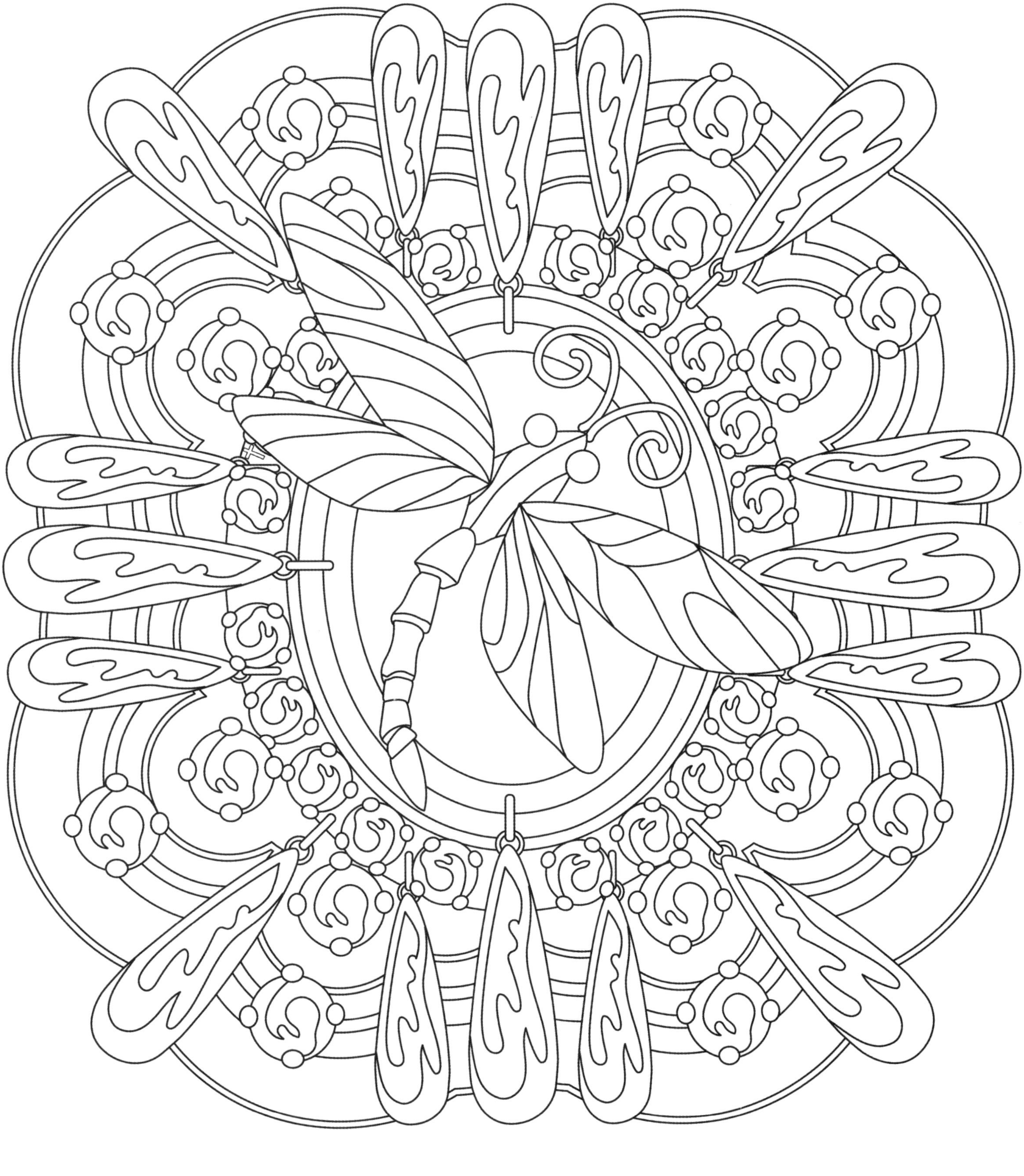

Be careful for nothing; but in every thing by prayer and supplication with thanksgiving let your requests be made known unto God.

Philippians 4:6

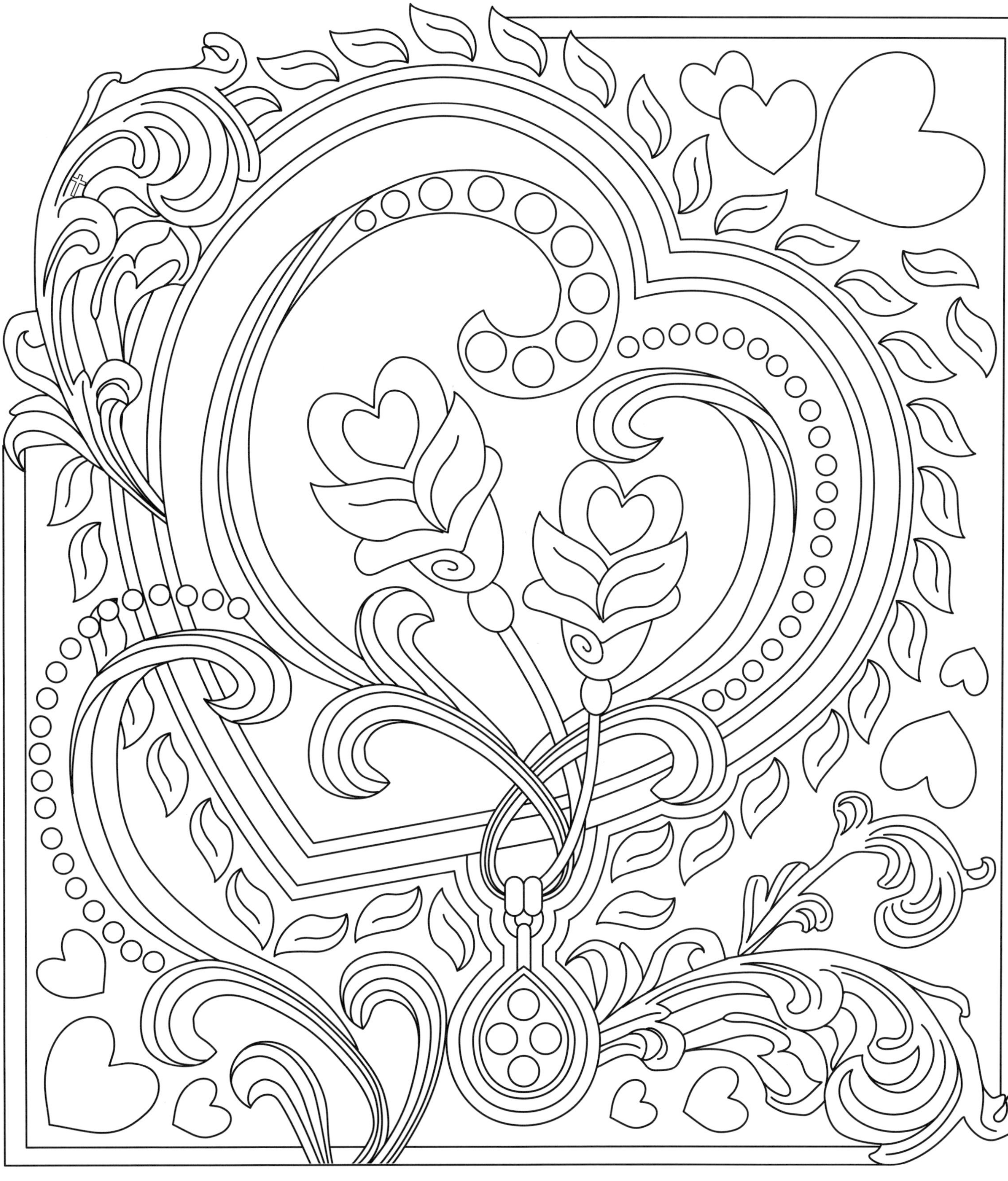

Husbands, love your wives, even as Christ also loved the church,
and gave himself for it.
Ephesians 5:25

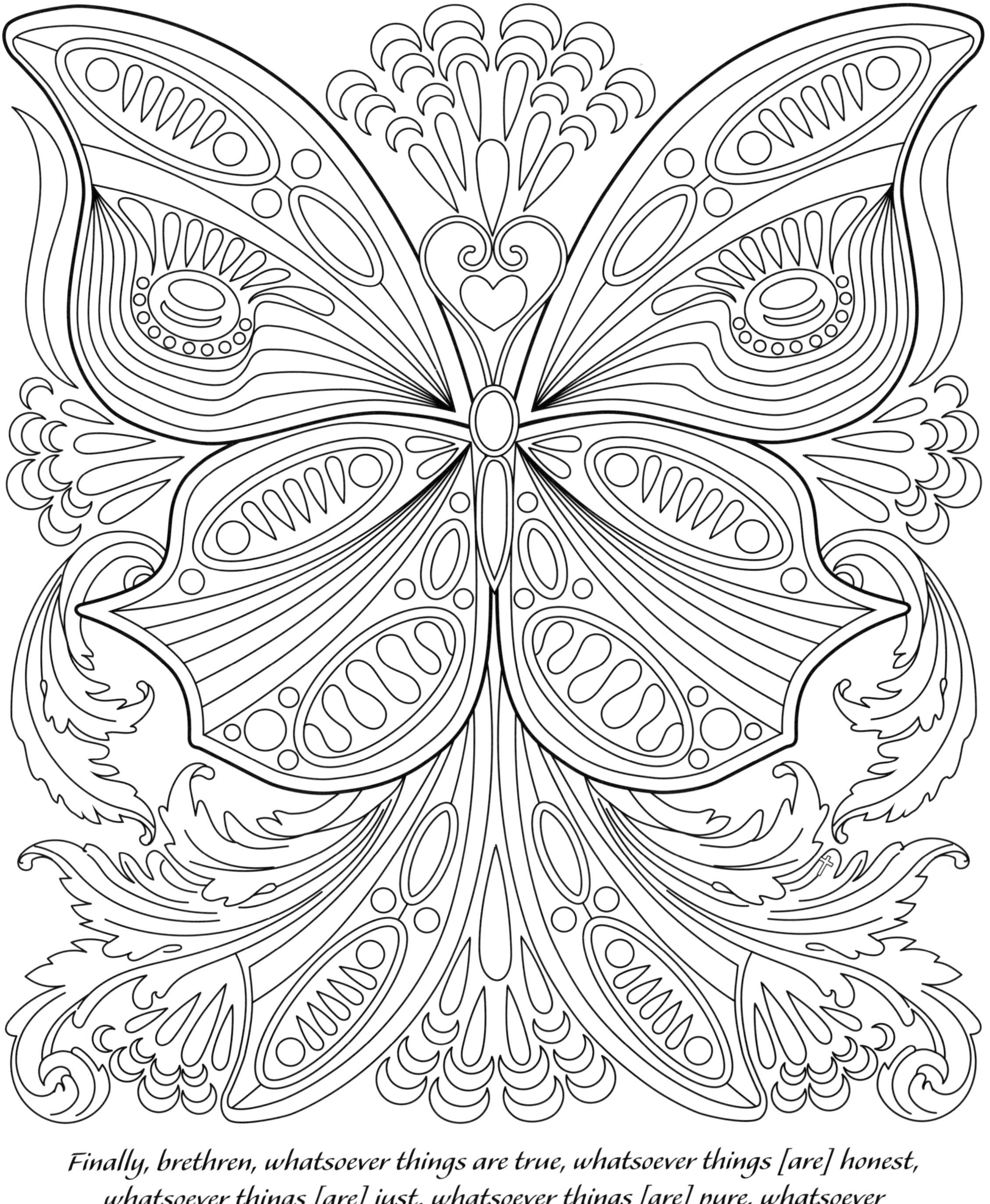

Finally, brethren, whatsoever things are true, whatsoever things [are] honest, whatsoever things [are] just, whatsoever things [are] pure, whatsoever things [are] lovely, whatsoever things [are] of good report; if [there be] any virtue, and if [there be] any praise, think on these things.

Philippians 4:8

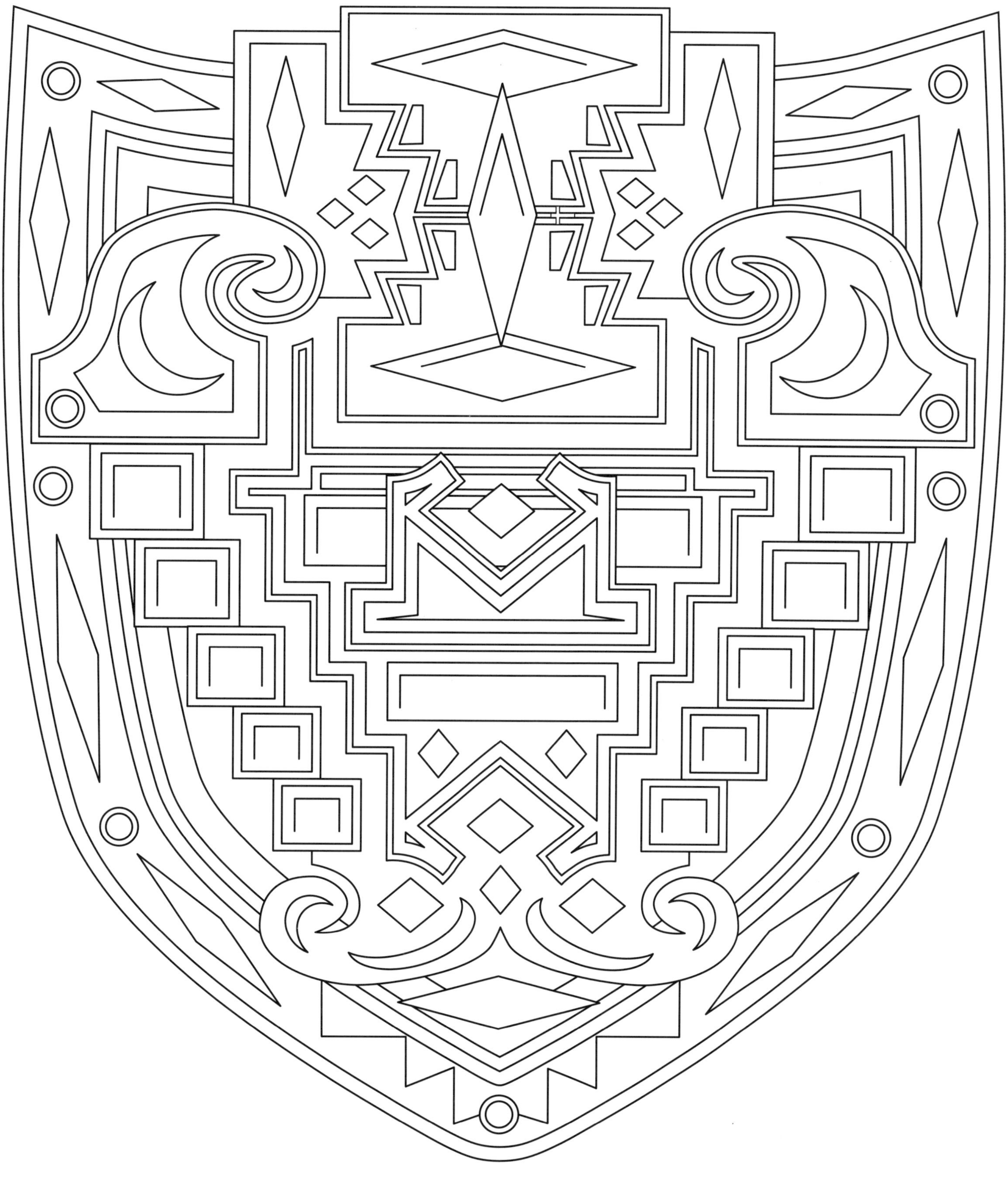

The LORD [is] my light and my salvation; whom shall I fear?
the LORD [is] the strength of my life; of whom shall I be afraid?
Psalm 27:1

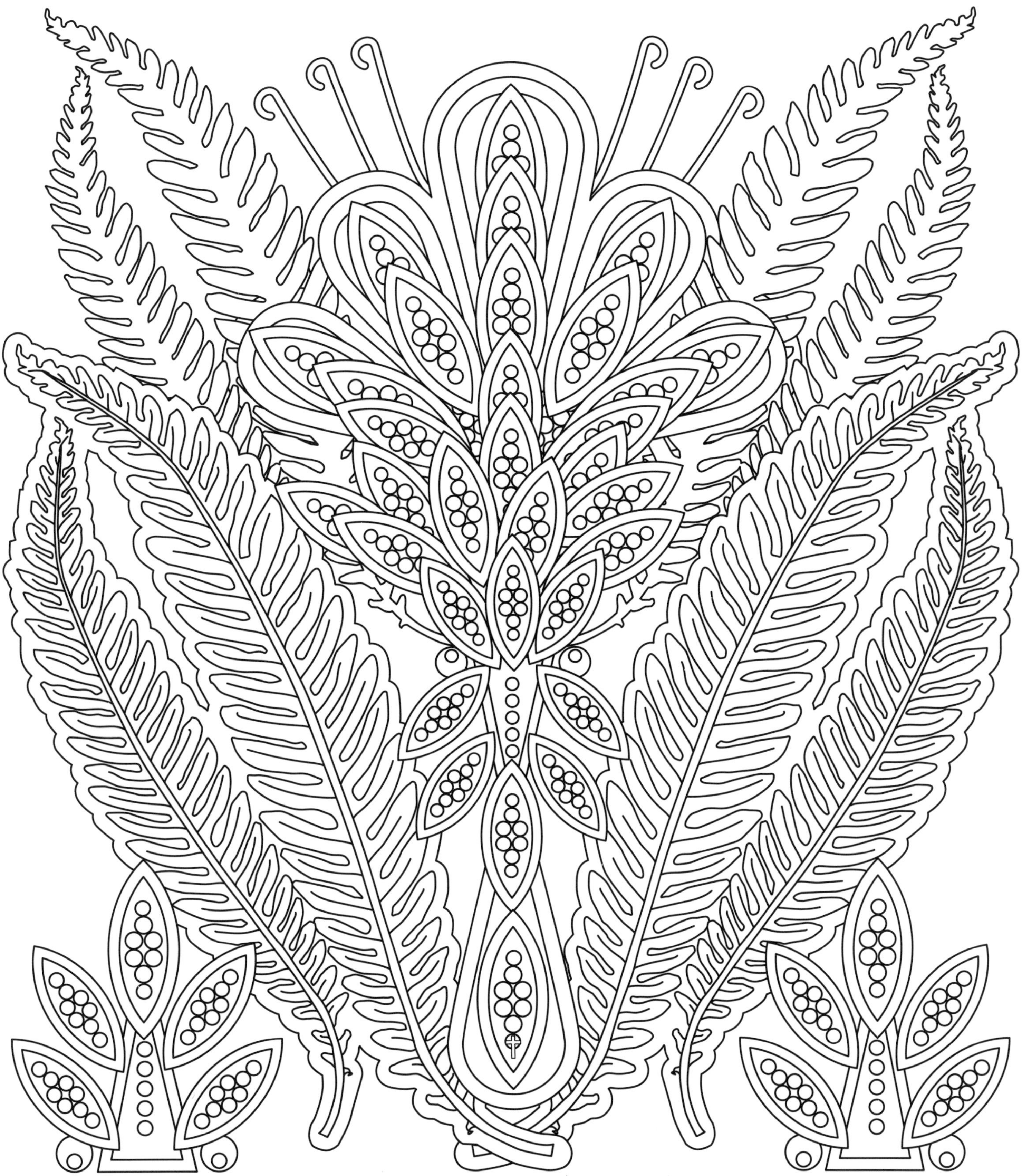

[There is] therefore now no condemnation to them which are in Christ Jesus, who walk not after the flesh, but after the Spirit.

Romans 8:1

A new commandment I give unto you, That ye love one another;
as I have loved you, that ye also love one another.
John 13:34

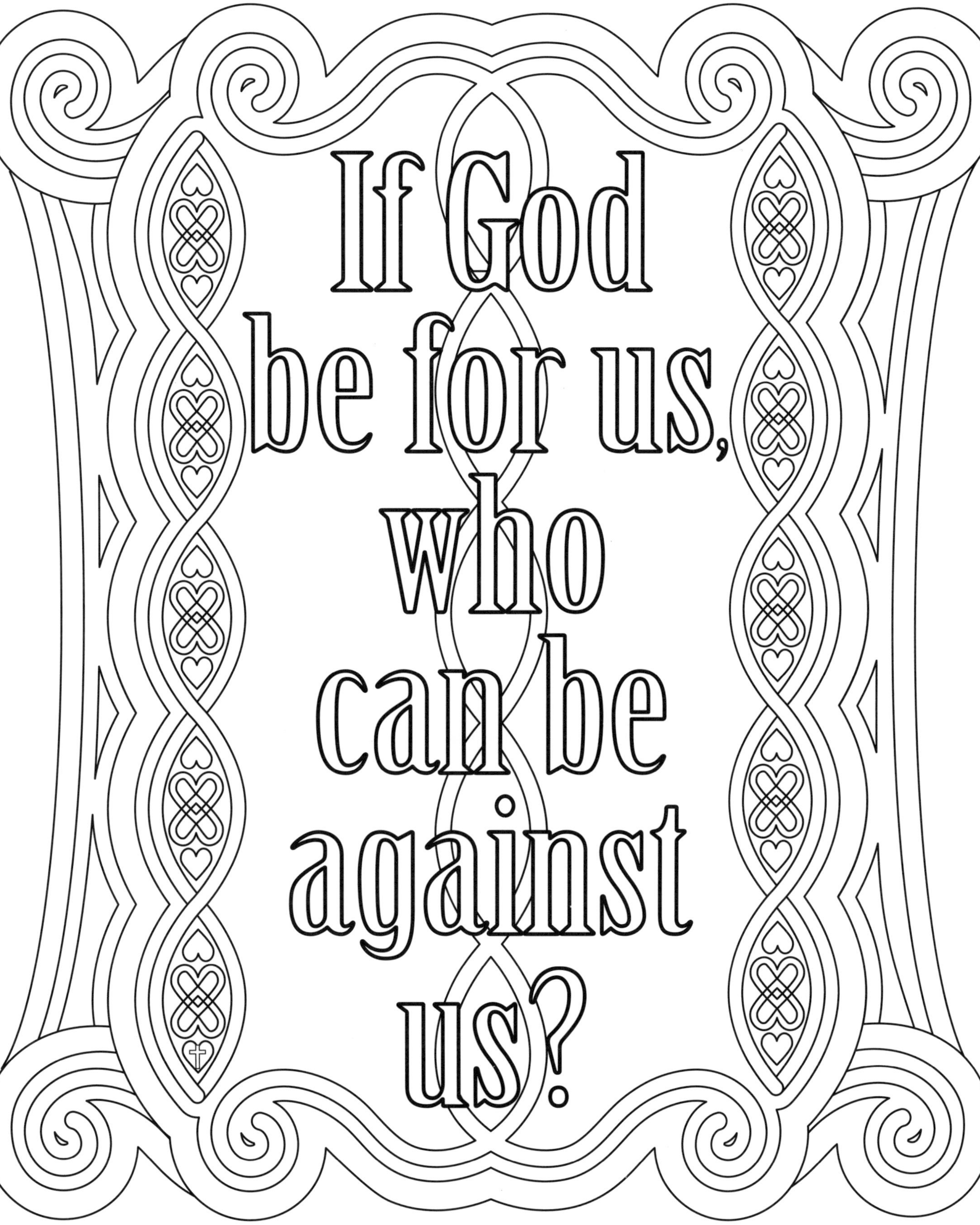

If God be for us, who can be against us?
Romans 8:31

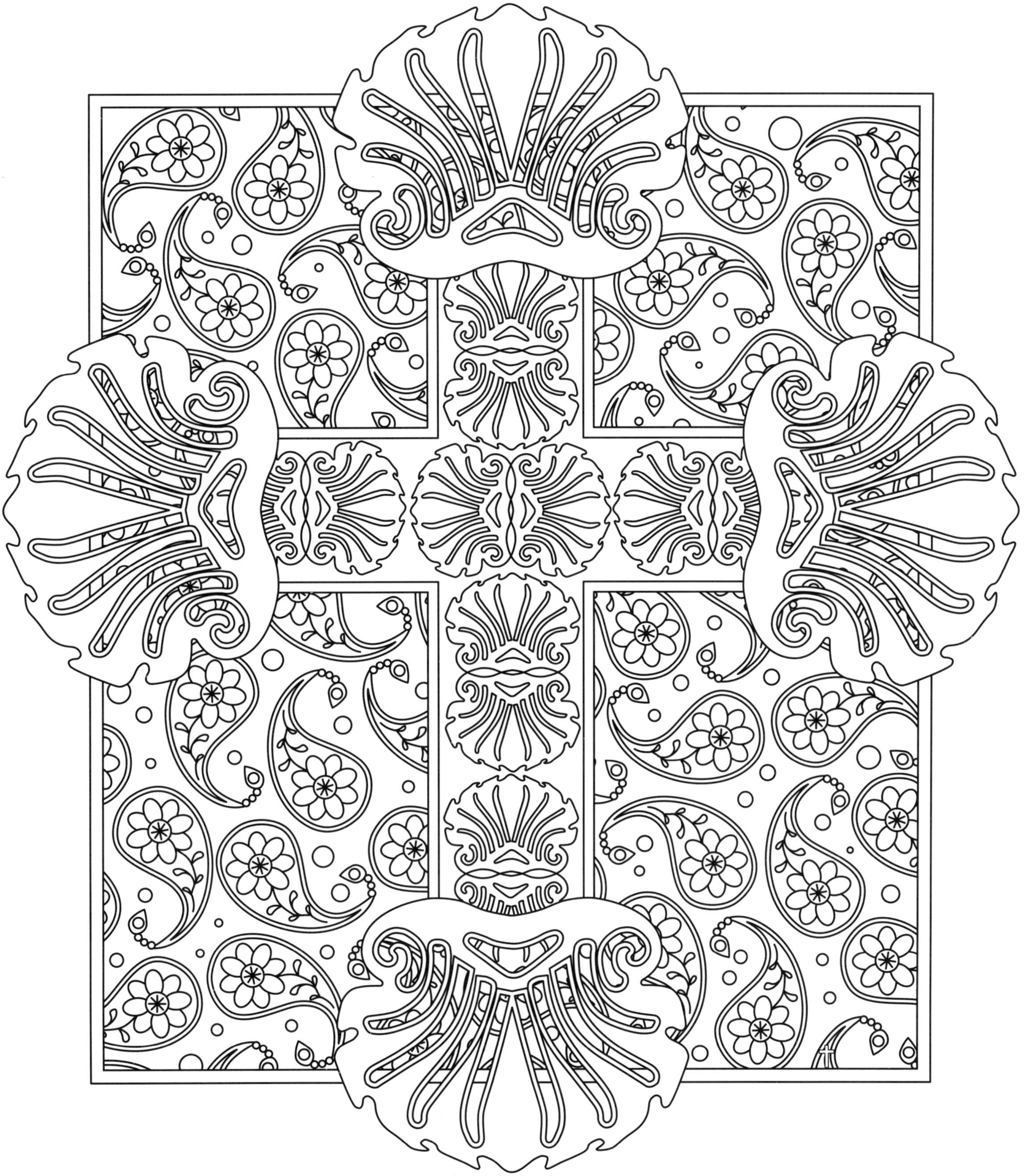

And now, little children, abide in him; that, when he shall appear,
we may have confidence, and not be ashamed before him at his coming.
1 John 2:28

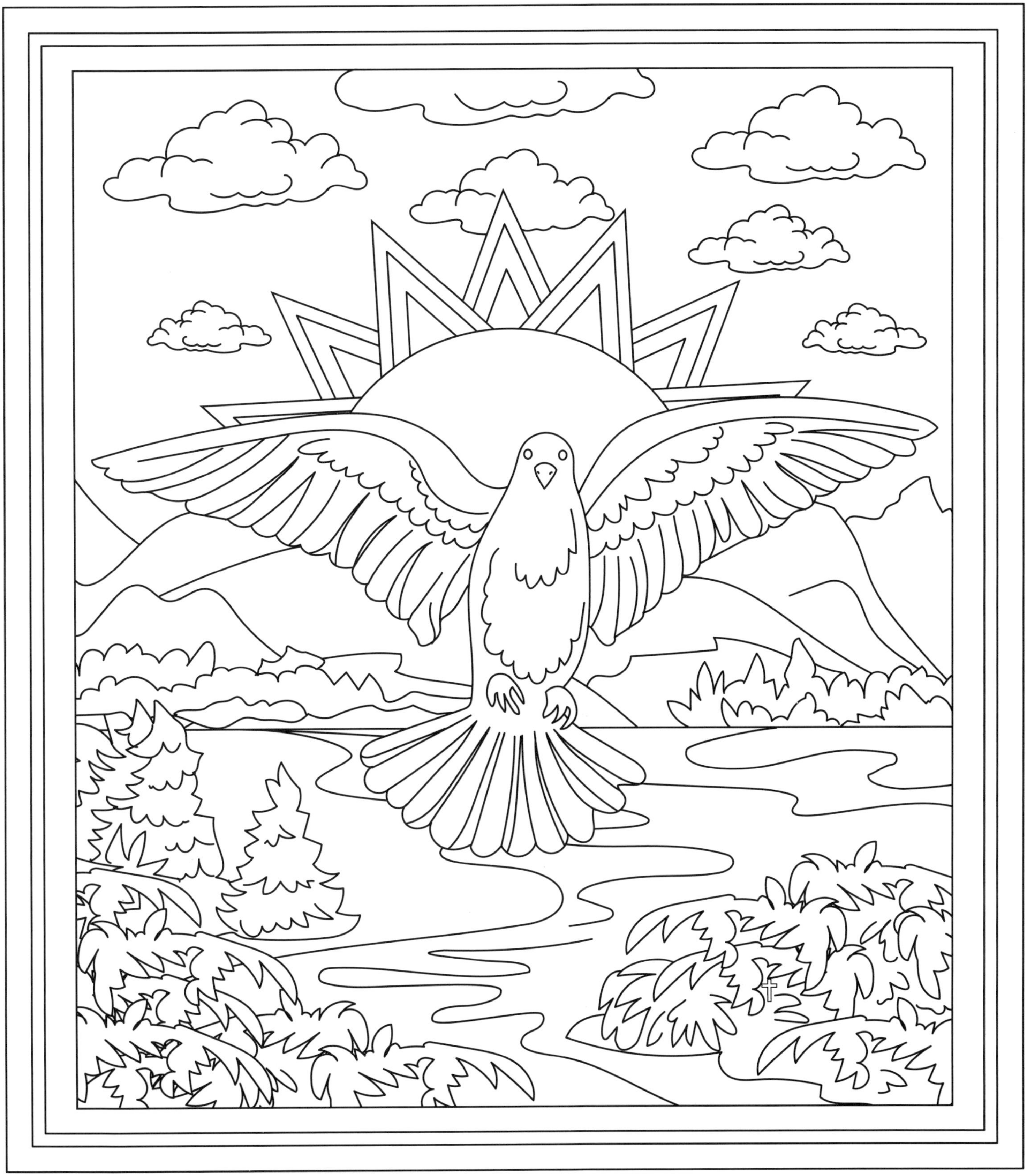

Blessed [are] the peacemakers: for they shall be called the children of God.
Matthew 5:9

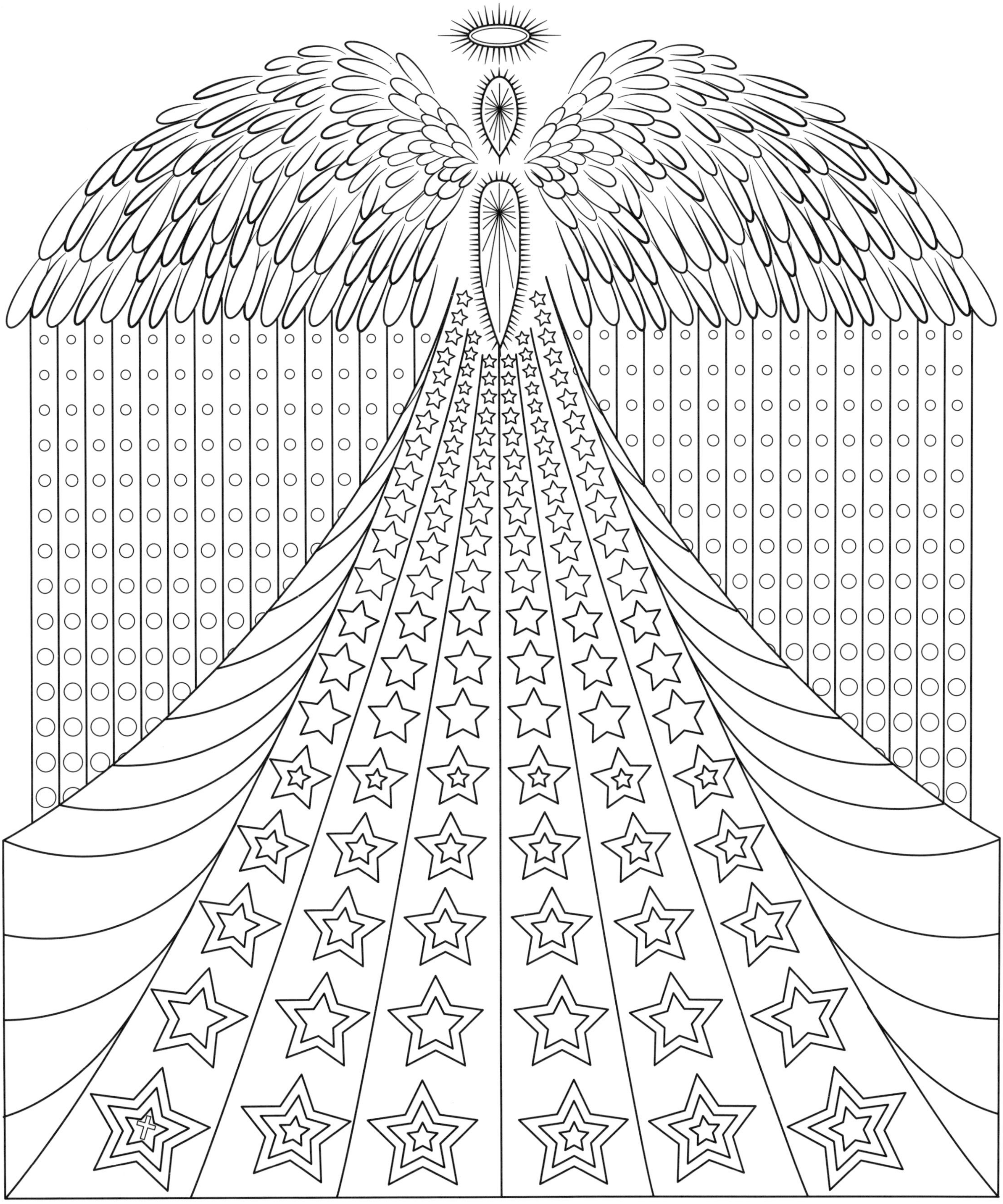

And the angel said unto them, Fear not: for, behold,
I bring you good tidings of great joy.
Luke 2:10